lonely 🌏 planet

PO

T0022722

ATHENS

TOP EXPERIENCES • LOCAL LIFE

ALEXIS AVERBUCK

Contents

Plan Your Trip 4

Temple of Olympian Zeus (p118)
MARINA PLUG/SHUTTERSTOCK ©

Welcome to Athens

By Alexis Averbuck, Writer

Athens in the early morning is a treat to behold. When I visit, I always make sure to explore during those quiet initial hours when the stores are just opening, the views are unobstructed and the air is cool. Then, as the day heats up, along with the action, catch the ride: through elegant museums, chaotic shopping streets, verdant oases, all surrounding that impeccable monument, the Acropolis. The other extreme, the night, is when the city's world-class restaurant and bar scene comes alive – better hope you've had a siesta.

The Acropolis and Parthenon Temple

SVEN HANSCHE/SHUTTERSTOCK

Top Experiences

Explore ancient Greece at the Acropolis (p36)

PETR F. MAREK/SHUTTERSTOCK ©

R. NAGY/SHUTTERSTOCK ©

Examine treasures at the Acropolis Museum (p44)

Step into the past at the Ancient Agora (p58)

GEORGIOS TSICHLIS /SHUTTERSTOCK ©

SAIKO3P/SHUTTERSTOCK ©

Immerse yourself at the Benaki Museum of Greek Culture (p102)

Admire antiquities at the National Archaeological Museum (p130)

HERACLES KRITIKOS/SHUTTERSTOCK ©

Wander the ruins at Kerameikos (p158)

Stroll up Filopappou Hill (p148)

Marvel at the Temple of Olympian Zeus (p118)

Dining Out

Eating, drinking and talking are the main entertainment for Athenians. The current restaurant scene is vibrant, and some of the best cooking is found in just-slightly modernised tavernas that showcase fresh produce and regional ingredients. Add in a culture of convivial alfresco dining, and no wonder meals tend to last for hours.

Restaurant Types

Tavernas are neighbourhood anchors. A *psarotaverna* focuses on seafood; a *hasapotaverna* or *psistaria* does meat. Also casual, a *mayirio* specialises in home-style stews and baked dishes *(mayirefta)*. More formal is the *estiatorio*, with cloth on the tables.

Casual *ouzeries* and *mezedhopoleia* both serve small plates with drinks. Souvlaki (aka *kalamaki*) is Athens' favourite fast food; restaurants that do these grilled meat skewers usually also do *gyros* (slivers of meat cooked on a vertical rotisserie).

What Looks Good

In summer, an empty room doesn't necessarily mean bad – it could just be that everyone is on the roof terrace or in the courtyard.

At family-run places, it's normal to go into the kitchen to see the day's dishes.

For other tips on ordering, see Menu Advice.

Best Traditional Greek

Karamanlidika tou Fani The corner butcher, reimagined as a restaurant. (p68)

Aspro Alogo Simple taverna smack in the middle of downtown. (p90)

Diporto Agoras Legendary cheap lunch spot near the central market. (p77)

I Kriti Super-rustic Cretan specialities. (p138)

Atlantikos The freshest seafood, simply prepared. (p68)

Best Mezedhes

Ivis Watch the Psyrri scene from a little table at this sweet corner bar-cafe. (p70)

Glykys Complement ouzo with meatballs, spicy sausages and other classics

RAWF8/SHUTTERSTOCK ©

at this Plaka courtyard spot. (p90)

Atitamos Laid-back spot in Exarhia for delish small plates. (p138)

Ama Lachei stis Nefelis At this converted school you'll learn about the vast variety of seasonal Greek food. (p138)

Best Modern Greek

Soil High-concept, creative, contemporary tasting menus. (p124)

Merceri Food & Drink Thisio's entry, with Mediterranean flair. (p152)

Mavro Provato The best of Athens' modern tavernas. (p124)

Spondi A beautiful garden setting and Michelin-lauded food. (p125)

CTC Urban Gastronomy Ambitious mystery tasting menus. (p165)

Best Snacks and Sweets

Elvis Excellent-quality meat goes into the skewers at this rockin' souvlaki joint. (p166)

Feyrouz Fresh, healthy and spicy – a budget diner's best friend. (p63)

Kallimarmaro Spinach and cheese pies, cookies and treats, made in the most traditional way. (p125)

Cremino Sumptuous gelato and sorbet. (p90)

Kostas Eat your souvlaki standing. (p69)

Eating Etiquette

○ Athenians start eating dinner around 9pm.

○ For trendy restaurants, book ahead on weekends (try www.e-table.gr) or go early.

○ Plates are typically not cleared until you ask for the bill (and you must ask for it).

Bar Open

In Athens the line between cafe and bar is blurry. Most places segue from coffee to drinks, and maybe music and a DJ, at night. There is usually food – although places that serve only drinks have become more common. The smoking ban is often ignored.

Neighbourhoods

Gazi and Kolonaki tend towards slicker, spendier clubs. For cheaper drinks and live music, head for Keramikos or Exarhia. Psyrri and north of Syntagma are the best central areas for interesting bars.

Greek Music

Traditional music pops up all over. Bars and tavernas – especially in Plaka, Psyrri and Exarhia – host bands evenings and Sunday afternoons.

More formal clubs operate September to May, start around 11.30pm and do not have a cover charge (though drinks are pricier than in bars).

Summer Clubs

In summer, Athenians decamp to mega-clubs along the seafront in Glyfada, along the tramline. If you book for dinner you don't pay cover; otherwise, admission ranges from €10 to €20 and includes one drink. Glam up to get in.

Best Neighbourhood Bars

Six d.o.g.s. One of the best in Psyrri: indoor-outdoor, rooms upon rooms. (p72)

Chelsea Hotel Pangrati-style chill, packed day and night. (p126)

Galaxy Bar A gorgeous old vintage space, hidden in a Syntagma arcade. (p81)

Dude Bar Late-night with great grooves. (p71)

Nabokov Low-key literati spot on the edge of Exarhia. (p142)

Alphaville The Keramikos (night) lifestyle in a nutshell. (p161)

Blue Parrot Metaxourgio staple on Plateia Avdi. (p168)

SUN_SHINE/SHUTTERSTOCK ©

Best Speciality Bars

Baba Au Rum Takes umbrella drinks seriously. (p91)

The Clumsies Repeatedly cited for world's best bartenders. (p91)

Heteroclito Lovely unpretentious wine bar. (p91)

Barley Cargo The Greek beer experts. (p91)

Best Cafes

Taf Coffee House roasted, perfectly brewed. (p142)

Buñuel Uptempo Bistro A newer name in Kolonaki. (p112)

Little Tree Book Cafe Coffee, wine and snacks with local bookworms. (p50)

To Tsai For the tea lovers of the world. (p112)

Best Photo Ops

Couleur Locale The Acropolis looks close enough to touch at this rooftop bar. (p74)

Little Kook The view in this case is not the Acropolis, but the wild decor. (p73)

Noel Everyone looks photogenic in this beautifully lit bar. (p72)

Yiasemi Look at you, sipping a drink on the most scenic steps in Plaka! (p92)

Nightlife Tips

• Bars begin filling after 11pm and usually stay open till 2am, or 4am on weekends.

• Public transport stops or slows after midnight, but cabs are very cheap.

Treasure Hunt

Central Athens is the city's original commercial district, and one big shopping hub, with an eclectic mix of stores. The area is still organised roughly by category – lace and buttons on one block, light bulbs on the next. The main (if generic) shopping street is pedestrianised Ermou, running from Syntagma to Monastiraki.

Style Hunting

As with many creative endeavours in Athens, fashion and design are flourishing. For the shopper who wants what no one else has yet, Alternative Athens (p22) runs tours of designers' workshops.

Sales & Pricing

The big months for sales are mid-January to February and mid-July to August, especially on clothes, with additional mid-season sales in the first 10 days of May and November. Bargaining is accept- able at flea markets, and perhaps gently at dustier antiques dealers, but in general prices are fixed.

Best Creative Souvenirs

Korres Stock up on this Greek beauty brand. (p96)

Forget Me Not The original dealer in smart souvenirs and other cool design items, all with a Hellenic twist. (p94)

Flâneur Love feta? Show your loyalty with a cute pin or patch. (p94)

TAF This gallery-cafe also has a very cool design shop. (p68)

Benaki Museum at 138 Pireos Street The gift shop at this contemporary art museum is top-notch. (p163)

Best Arts and Crafts

Amorgos Handmade pup- pets and toys. (p96)

Benaki Museum of Greek Culture Excellent handicrafts in the gift shop. (p102)

Zoumboulakis Gallery Prints of work by some of Greece's finest artists. (p112)

Chrisanthos Spread the worry-bead habit with a set from this old shop. (p63)

Monastiraki Flea Market Dusty treasures are waiting to be discovered. (p63)

Eleni Marneri Galerie Local modern art and super jewellery. (p96)

JOSE HERNANDEZ CAMERA 51/SHUTTERSTOCK ©

Best Accessories

Lemisios Classic shoe shop that can customise its designs. (p114)

Katerina Ioannidis Delicate jewellery with a folkloric touch. (p114)

Melissinos Art The (son of the) 'poet sandal maker' is an Athens legend. (p53)

Zacharias Lovely leather goods screen-printed with ancient patterns. (p144)

Best Food

Varvakios Agora Maybe you don't need a whole lamb, but you do need to see the city's central market. (p77)

Exarhia Weekly Market Athens' neighbourhood veg markets are a treat; this is a great one. (p142)

Pantopoleion Kolios Much more than the usual grocery store, this shop stocks excellent regional items. (p77)

Mastiha Shop All kinds of products featuring the miracle resin mastic. (p114)

Best Music

Yiannis Samouelan Best bouzoukis in town. (p74)

Xylouris Traditional Cretan music, instruments and general knowledge. (p97)

Plan 59 Especially good selection of Greek vinyl. (p144)

Typical Shop Hours

○ Normal closing (5pm or so): Monday, Wednesday, Saturday.

○ Late (8pm, sometimes with an afternoon break): Tuesday, Thursday, Friday.

○ Exception: Plaka tourist shops, always open late.

Show Time

The Athens arts and music scene depends largely on the season: many big halls and theatres close or scale back in the summer, when open-air spaces take over. Bonus: Greeks consider every musical event an opportunity for a singalong, which can make the most formal concert venues feel chummy (even if you don't know the words).

Athens Epidaurus Festival

June to August is time for this world-class festival (p22) of local and international music, dance and drama at the ancient Odeon of Herodes Atticus at the Acropolis. It's absolutely worth planning around.

Open-Air Cinema

One of the delights of Athens is watching the latest Hollywood or art-house flick in the warm summer air. The settings are old-fashioned gardens and rooftops, with modern sound and projection. Cinemas start up in early May and usually close in September. For movie times, see **Athinorama** (www.athinorama. gr), which has a filter for outdoor theatres; use a browser translator, as it's Greek only.

Listings & Tickets

Check the **Kathimerini English Edition** (www.ekathimerini. com), which is also a print supplement to the *International New York Times*, and **This**
Is Athens (www.this isathens.gr). Greek site ελ**culture** (www. elculture.gr) is more comprehensive. **Viva** (www.viva.gr) is a major ticket vendor.

Best Multiuse Spaces

Gazarte Multiple venues in this big building in Gazi. (p168)

TAF A cluster of 19th-century buildings with a great courtyard cafe. (p68)

Treno sto Rouf A cool bar and cabaret, plus occasional creative performance, in old rail cars. (p169)

Bios Industrial chic with a cinema, a gallery, a bar and more. (p169)

PIT STOCK/SHUTTERSTOCK © ARCHITECT: RENZO PIANO BUILDING WORKSHOP

Best
Big Venues

National Theatre English-language surtitles for many performances. (p143)

Technopolis Open-air music hall in the converted gasworks. (p169)

Stavros Niarchos Foundation Cultural Center Tonnes of programming year-round here, including the Greek National Opera. (p171)

Best
Live Music

Afrikana Jazz and world music in a small converted house. (p169)

O Kavouras *Rembetika* (blues songs) club in Exarhia. (p144)

Half Note Jazz Club The city's premier jazz venue. (p127)

Feidiou 2 Music Cafe Informal and intimate. (p143)

Best Open-Air
Cinemas

Cine Paris Claims to be the oldest open-air cinema, in a prime Plaka location. (p94)

Cine Dexameni In a leafy square in Kolonaki. (p114)

Thission The Acropolis view competes for attention. (p155)

Riviera Eclectic and artsy programming at this Exarhia favourite. (p143)

Worth a Trip

The city's state-of-the-art concert hall, **Megaron Mousikis** (www.megaron.gr), presents a rich winter program of operas and concerts. In summer it has shows in the back garden. The Music Library of Greece is also located here, with some 10,000 sound recordings.

Museums & History

Without a doubt, Athens' top draw is its ancient ruins and the blockbuster museums dedicated to this same period. But a city this old has many more layers of history, and many other critical artistic moments – along with excellent museums, churches and other patches of hallowed ground.

Best Art Museums

National Archaeological Museum The world's best collection of Ancient Greek art. (p130)

National Gallery Brand-new, sparkling complex of Greek painting. (p122)

Basil & Elise Goulandris Foundation Top art collection in gorgeous galleries. (p122)

Benaki Museum at 138 Pireos Street Rotating exhibits of primarily modern and contemporary art in a converted industrial space. (p163)

National Museum of Contemporary Art In a remodelled brewery, see contemporary Greek and international art stars. (p47)

Museum of Cycladic Art Connecting ancient art with modern, featuring the minimalist sculptures that inspired Picasso and Modigliani. (p108)

Best Historical Sites

Acropolis Obviously! With its accompanying museum. (p38)

Theatre of Dionysos The birthplace of theatre, on the Acropolis' southern slopes. (p43)

Ancient Agora Ancient Athens' heart, the lively hub of administrative, commercial, political and social activity. (p58)

Hill of the Pnyx Ancient Athens' democratic assembly met and debated here. (p151)

National Historical Museum In the old Parliament building, where Prime Minister Theodoros Deligiannis was assassinated on the front steps in 1905. (p86)

Aristotle's Lyceum Where the famed philosopher led his students on thoughtful walks. (p109)

Best Speciality Museums

Byzantine & Christian Museum Is it art? Is it culture? It's simply beautiful. (p108)

STORM IS ME/SHUTTERSTOCK ©

Jewish Museum Explore the deep roots of Greek Jews. (p85)

Museum of Islamic Art Jaw-droppingly beautiful art from the Middle East and Asia. (p163)

Best Byzantine Churches

Church of Agios Dimitrios Loumbardiaris Site of an alleged miracle in 1648, when a lightning strike is said to have saved the congregation from Turkish attack. (p149)

Church of Agios Eleftherios Look for the nude pagan relief on the north outside wall. (p67)

Church of Sotira Lykodimou Built in the 11th century, with 19th-century icons. (p86)

Need To Know

∘ Outside of peak summer, most sites and museums close by early afternoon – and small museums may have limited hours year-round. Confirm hours before setting out.

∘ Churches have no set opening times; just duck in whenever you see one open.

∘ Eligible for reduced entrance? See Discount Cards (p172).

Activities & Events

With its winding streets, Athens rewards random wandering and unstructured exploration. But top-notch tour guides and enriching activities can help you dig deeper, and special events can shape your itinerary too. Activities that don't require pre-planning are listed in the relevant chapters.

KOSTAS TSEK/SHUTTERSTOCK ©

Best Tours

This Is My Athens (www.thisisathens.org/withalocal) City-run program pairs you with a volunteer local. Book 72 hours ahead.

Alternative Athens (www.alternativeathens.com; tours from €40) As the name implies, tours with less-typical slants.

Roll in Athens (www.rollinathens.tours) Take a bike tour around the centre – or better still, down to the seaside.

Solebike (www.solebike.eu) See the sights on an electric bike.

Best Arts Events

Athens Epidaurus Festival (https://aefestival.gr) Since 1955, Athens' premier arts event, set in an ancient theatre.

Athens Biennale (http://athensbiennale.org) Every two years, showcasing top local and international artists.

Athens Jazz (www.athensjazz.gr) Week-long free festival in Gazi in May or June.

August Moon Festival On the night of the full moon, ancient sites stay open late and host music.

Best Food Activities

Athens Walking Tours (www.athenswalkingtours.gr) Its cooking class shows how to roll your own filo for *spanakopita* (spinach pie).

Athens Street Food Festival (https://athensstreetfoodfestival.gr) Instantly popular when it started in 2016.

Cycle Greece (☎210 921 8160; www.cyclegreece.com) Runs a day bike tour of Athens-area wineries.

Under the Radar Athens

MILAN GONDA/SHUTTERSTOCK ©

Once one of the most desirable addresses in Athens, Kypseli is still home to some neoclassical and art deco gems. Street art abounds, so join a walking tour if you want to see some funky offerings before stopping off in one of the traditional family tavernas.

Kypseli

Kypseli, a 15-minute walk north of Exarhia, was once one of the most desirable residential areas of Athens, on a par with Kolonaki. It's not so ritzy today, even though if you keep an eye out there's still the odd pretty neoclassical mansion or art deco block to be found among the dense streets of identikit five-storey Athens apartment blocks.

The neighbourhood's social centre is the Fokionos Negri pedestrian strip of park, lined with cafes.

Kypseli Municipal Market (https://ago rakypselis.gr), a 1935 modernist building, houses a range of social projects including the non-profit business Wise Greece, which sells some 2500 high-quality food products.

Metaxourgio

Epic-scale street art abounds in Metaxourgio. To discover some of the best works join one of Alternative Athens' (p22)' excellent themed walking tours.
The Breeder (http://thebreeder system.com) is a hip concrete warehouse-style art gallery; every year it reinvents its exterior design as an art project.

Pangrati

Pangrati's Plateia Varnava is a great place to experience a typical Athenian neighbourhood, with families dining in the tavernas and kids playing in the square. Buy a snack from the bakery Kallimarmaro (p125) and a soft drink from the *periptero* (kiosk) and sit and enjoy the scene.

LGBTIQ+

KOSTAS KOUTSAFTIKIS/SHUTTERSTOCK ©

Greece's reputation as a millennia-old gay-friendly culture sometimes clashes with contemporary Orthodox mores: gay marriage is not yet legal, for example. But Athens' LGBTIQ+ scene is lively and increasingly becoming an international draw. Athens Pride, held in June, has been an annual event since 2005.

Neighbourhoods

For nightlife, Gazi is Athens' main gay and lesbian hub, with both a few big mega-clubs and, more on the fringes of the area, some good small bars.

Gay-friendly cafes can also be found around Plateia Agia Irini and in Metaxourgio and Exarhia. Alternative Athens (p22) runs a bar crawl tour around some of the neighbourhoods.

Best by Night

BeQueer The new generation of gay nightlife. (p168)

S-Cape Long-established mega-club in Gazi. (p168)

Noiz Club Also in Gazi, for women. (p161)

Big The main outpost of Athens' lively bear scene. (p168)

Koukles Old-school drag in Koukaki. (p52)

Best by Day

Myrovolos A popular lesbian spot. Greek meals available. (p161)

Beaver Collective Women run this cafe by the Benaki Pireos annexe. (p168)

Rooster Cafe and cocktails in the centre of Monastiraki's booming scene, on Plateia Agia Irini. (p73)

Online Info

For more recommendations and events:

Athens Pride (www.athenspride.eu)

Athens Info Guide (www.athensinfoguide.com)

For Kids

ALEXANDROS MICHAILIDIS/SHUTTERSTOCK ©

Athens is short on playgrounds, but between ice cream and street musicians and giant ruins, there's plenty to keep kids amused. It helps too that children are welcome everywhere; at casual restaurants they're often encouraged to run off and play together while the adults eat.

Movie Magic

Outdoor cinema makes even a Hollywood blockbuster special. Only films for the youngest kids are dubbed; everything else gets Greek subtitles.

Shadow Puppets

Younger children may enjoy Greece's shadow-puppet tradition. Shows are in Greek, but it's really all about the slapstick comedy and music.

Best Spectacles

Theatro Skion Tasou Konsta Shadow-puppet theatre in the kid-friendly Flisvos Park; moves to Plaka in winter. (p171)

Melina Merkouri Cultural Centre Shadow-puppet shows on Sundays year-round. (p152)

Cine Paris Lovely open-air movies, right in the centre. (p94)

Best Parks and Gardens

National Gardens A playground, duck pond and bare-bones zoo. (p85)

Filopappou Hill Thrilling views of the Acropolis. (p148)

Stavros Niarchos Park Grand modern park south of the centre; rent a bike to roam. (p171)

Lykavittos Hill Admire the whole city from the peak. Bonus: novelty funicular ride. (p105)

Latraac Skate park meets cafe. (p165)

Best Museums and Tours

Museum of Greek Children's Art Dedicated space for exhibiting young artists' work. (p88)

Athens Happy Train All aboard this mini tour bus/train. (p88)

Responsible Travel

Life in Athens can be tough; as a visitor, there are opportunities to tune in to what is going on and do what you can to help ease the impact of your presence, as well as contribute to the value of life in the city.

Learn about Issues of the Day

Read up on local news and current events. The daily paper *Kathemerini* has an English-language edition (www.ekathimerini.com). Athens has a strong contingent of independent bookshops with a social responsibility edge.

Find out what local advocates are up to. Fenix Humanitarian Legal Aid (www.fenixaid.org), for example, works to support the needs of refugees.

Pay attention to street art. Across the city, from Exarhia to Psyrri, Gazi and Mets, you will encounter graffiti and street art, much of which proffers a point of view.

Leave a Light Footprint

Take the metro or even a bike. A cycling route runs from Thisio to the coast. Several outfits offer bicycle hire, such as Funky Ride (p177) and Solebike (p22).

Visit sustainably designed places. Covering a human-made slope that incorporates the roof of the Cultural Center, the Stavros Niarchos Park (p171) has been sustainably designed with paths cutting through plantings of lavender, olive trees and other Mediterranean flora.

Conserve water. At your accommodation reuse your bath towels rather than have them changed each day.

Support Local

Pick products that help. Wise Greece (www.wisegreece.com) products donate a percentage of the profit to buy food for people in need – you'll find them at the Kypseli Municipal Market (p23) – and Waterbags

R NAGY/SHUTTERSTOCK

(www.waterbags.gr) are widely available.

Shop at weekly laïki markets to support local producers. These street markets (http://laikesagores.gr) pop up in neighbourhoods once per week.

Look for outfits that take a role in local initiatives. Art gallery Breeder (p23) is active in community affairs.

Give Back

Dine or shop at a local non-profit. Support Shedia, a social and environmental project providing education, training and

jobs for the homeless and people living in poverty, by dining at Shedia Home (p74).

Buy from local creators. With tourism the only booming part of the economy, artists and designers have turned their creativity to Greece-themed products. Check out the wares at Athena Design Workshop (www.athenadesign workshop.com) and Koukoutsi (p144).

Try for sustainably made products. Increasingly, ranges of products, especially cosmetics and wellness lines, are being sustainably made: find them

at Apivita (www.apivita. com), Korres (p96) and Michalis Alexandrakis (p115).

Avoid Overtourism

Visit September to April to avoid the summer season peak.

Arrive at the sights when they open, or wait until towards the end of the day so you don't add to congestion.

Take advantage of green spaces, such as Filopappou Hill (p148), Lykavittos Hill (p105), National Gardens (p85), Stavros Niarchos Park (p171) and Strefi Hill (p135).

Four Perfect Days

Day 1

VIACHESLAV LOPATIN/SHUTTERSTOCK ©

Orient yourself by circling the centre, starting early at the **Acropolis** (pictured; p38). Then, wind down to the **Roman Agora** (p66) and the **Ancient Agora** (p58). Lunch at souvlaki legend **O Thanasis** (p71) or taverna **Maiandros** (p70), then shop along Plaka's **Adrianou Street**.

Then head to the **Acropolis Museum** (p44) and its masterpieces. At sundown, join the crowds strolling on Dionysiou Areopagitou, and walk up **Filopappou Hill** (p148). Dine with an Acropolis view at **Strofi** (p48) or on Peloponnesian fare at **Mani Mani** (p48).

Catch an outdoor movie at **Thission** (p155) or **Cine Paris** (p94) in Plaka. In cooler weather have a cosy drink at **Brettos** (p91) or **Hitchcocktales** (p51).

Day 2

HALAWI/SHUTTERSTOCK ©

First things first: the treasures of the **National Archaeological Museum** (p130). Then head back to the centre to the **Tomb of the Unknown Soldier** (pictured; p84) and watch the *evzones* (guards) strut their pom-pom-toed stuff.

Stroll south through the **National Gardens** (p85) to the old **Panathenaic Stadium** (p122), then pass by the **Temple of Olympian Zeus** (p118) and **Hadrian's Arch** (p55).

Have dinner in Pangrati at **Mavro Provato** (p124) or **Soil** (p124), then hit city-centre bars like **The Clumsies** (p91), **Six d.o.g.s.** (p72) or **Noel** (p72).

Day 3

KIRILL SKOROBOGATKO/SHUTTERSTOCK ©

Explore the **Athens Central Market** (pictured; p76) and the surrounding shopping streets. Have lunch at **Diporto Agoras** (p77) or **Karamanlidika tou Fani** (p68).

Head to Kolonaki for window shopping or museums: the **Benaki Museum of Greek Culture** (p102), **Museum of Cycladic Art** (p108) and **Byzantine & Christian Museum** (p108) are all excellent. Or hit the new **National Gallery** (p122) for a tour of Greek painting. At sunset, take the funicular up **Lykavittos Hill** (p105), then eat dinner back downhill at **Filippou** (p105) or **Oikeio** (p110).

End with cocktails at one of the excellent Syntagma-area bars, such as **Dude Bar** (p71) or **Baba Au Rum** (p91). If you prefer casual beers, try Psyrri.

Day 4

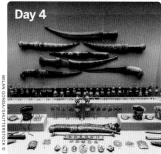

MILAN GONDA/SHUTTERSTOCK ©

Immerse yourself in the archaeological site of **Kerameikos** (p158), then visit the nearby **Museum of Islamic Art** (pictured; p163). Or if you're footsore from sightseeing, revive with a bath at **Hammam** (p164), then have lunch at **Ivis** (p70) or **Atlantikos** (p68).

Get a shot of contemporary art at **Benaki Museum at 138 Pireos Street** (p163). The cafe here is nice for coffee – or cross the road to **Upopa Epops** (p153). For dinner head up to Thisio's **Steki tou Ilia** (p152), **Merceri Food & Drink** (p152) or **CTC Urban Gastronomy** (p165) in Keramikos (book ahead).

Explore nightlife venues in Gazi: a DJ at **Gazarte** (p168) or **Bios** (p169), a jazz band at **Afrikana** (p169) or a sweaty late night in clubs like **BeQueer** (p168).

Need to Know

For detailed information, see Survival Guide (p172)

Population
City 664,000; wider municipality 3.1 million

Currency
Euro (€)

Language
Greek

Visas
Schengen rules apply; not required for stays of up to 90 days for many nationalities.

Money
Major banks have branches around Syntagma. ATMs only in commercial districts.

Time
Eastern European Time (GMT/UTC + two hours)

Phones
EU phones have free roaming. Or buy an inexpensive GSM SIM card at phone shops; bring your passport.

Tipping
If service charge added on restaurant bill, round to nearest euro. If not, tip 10% to 20%.

Daily Budget

Budget: Less than €130
Dorm bed: €32

Pension double: from €75

Souvlaki or *pita* (pie): €2.50

Ouzo with snack: €3

90-minute transit ticket: €1.20

Midrange: €130–250
Double in midrange hotel: €90–180

Traditional taverna meal: €15–17

Museum and site entry fees: €5–20

Taxi across town: €9

Top end: More than €250
Double room in top hotel: from €180

Trendy restaurant meal: from €30

Cocktail: €10

Acropolis tour guide: €75

Advance Planning

Three months before Reserve your hotel early, especially for summer.

One month before Check the cultural calendar and book tickets for a performance at the Greek National Opera, National Theatre or Megaron. Reserve a table at top restaurants.

One week before Check online to see if there'll be any strikes while you are there (www.apergia.gr is in Greek, so you'll need to translate it, or check the news page on the US Embassy website – https://gr.usembassy.gov); book tours and online tickets to the Acropolis.

Arriving in Athens

✈ Eleftherios Venizelos International Airport

In Spata, 27km east of Athens.

Metro €9, 50 minutes to Monastiraki, every 30 minutes, 6.30am to 11.30pm

Bus €5.50, one hour to 1½ hours to Syntagma, every 20 to 30 minutes, 24 hours

Taxi Flat fare to the centre day/night €40/55, 30 to 45 minutes

⚓ Port of Piraeus

Greece's main port, southwest of Athens.

Metro €1.20, 30 minutes to Thissio stop, 6.30am to 11.30pm

Regular Bus €1.20 from Piraeus to Syntagma in 50 minutes

Express Bus €4.10 from cruise ship terminal to Syntagma in 30 minutes, 7am to 9.15pm May to October only

Taxi €25 on the meter, 20 minutes

Getting Around

Central Athens is best explored on foot.

🚇 Metro

Three lines, wheelchair accessible. Runs 5am to midnight, till 2am Friday and Saturday in the centre.

🚌 Bus

Thorough, but no printed map; use Google Maps directions. Most useful: trolleybuses 2, 5, 11 and 15.

🚃 Tram

Scenic but slow way to the coast from Syntagma, 5.30am to 12.45am, till 1.40am Friday and Saturday in summer.

🚕 Taxi

Inexpensive. Hail or use apps **Beat** (www.thebeat.co/gr) or **Taxiplon** (www.taxiplon.gr). Surcharges for luggage; night/holiday rate is 60% higher.

Athens Neighbourhoods

Monastiraki & Psyrri (p56)
Busy Monastiraki and Psyrri are some of the city's liveliest quarters, with the wonderful Ancient Agora to the south.

Gazi, Keramikos & Metaxourgio (p156)
The industrial precinct of Gazi has been reborn as a club district, while Keramikos and Metaxourgio offer edgier nightlife and neighbourhood restaurants.

Filopappou Hill, Thisio & Petralona (p146)
Sweeping views of the Acropolis from Filopappou Hill, surrounded by the sedate and pleasant neighbourhoods of Thisio and Petralona.

Acropolis Area (p36)
Athens' crown is the Acropolis. This epic monument soars above the city, and on the hill's southern slopes, a fabulous modern museum holds its treasures.

Kerameikos ⊙

Ancient Agora ⊙

⊙ Acropolis

Acropolis Museum

Filopappou ⊙ Hill

Omonia & Exarhia (p128)

Omonia is home to the magnificent National Archaeological Museum, while nearby Exarhia has an interesting mix of students, activists and artists.

Kolonaki (p100)

Kolonaki is an adjective as much as a district: chic, stylish, elite. For visitors, it's also the location of several excellent museums and is a delightfully green area.

⊙ *National Archaeological Museum*

Syntagma & Plaka (p78)

Narrow streets, neoclassical mansions, Byzantine churches and tavernas, Plaka is ground zero for Athens tourism, while Syntagma is the heart of modern Athens.

⊙ *Benaki Museum of Greek Culture*

⊙   ⊙ *Temple of Olympian Zeus*

Mets & Pangrati (p116)

The attractive districts of Mets and Pangrati surround the Panathenaic Stadium, with unpretentious neighbourhoods and low-key-cool places to eat.

Explore
Athens

View from the Acropolis (p38) ADRIENNE PITTS/LONELY PLANET ©

Explore

Acropolis Area

Athens' crown is the Acropolis and its jewel is the Parthenon. This epic monument soars above the city, and on the hill's southern slopes, a modern museum holds its treasures. A promenade links the two – it's a tourist throughway, but also a favourite spot for locals to enjoy a sundown stroll. Further south, the neigh-bourhoods of Makrygianni and Koukaki deliver a slice of residential life.

The Short List

o **Acropolis (p38)** *Walking up the western slope of the temple-city, via marble stairs and ramps, as worshippers did some 2500 years ago.*

o **Parthenon (p39)** *Feeling like an ant, standing next to the columns of this iconic building synonymous with Ancient Greece.*

o **Acropolis Museum (p44)** *Feeling like a giant, as you look at the frieze from the top of the Parthenon, now installed on the top floor here.*

o **Odeon of Herodes Atticus (p47)** *Taking in a concert on a balmy summer night at this classical open-air theatre.*

o **Solebike (p22)** *Learning about Athens' sights on electric bikes.*

Getting There & Around

Ⓜ Akropoli (red line) sits near the Acropolis Museum and the Acropolis east entrance, just off the major boulevard Leoforos Syngrou.

Ⓜ Monastiraki (blue line) or Thissio (green line) stops are further away, a scenic walk to the Acropolis' western entrance.

Acropolis Area Map on p46

The Porch of the Caryatids, Acropolis MIRIAM GIMBEL/SHUTTERSTOCK ©

Top Experience 📷
Explore Ancient
Greece at the Acropolis

◉ MAP P46, B1

http://odysseus.culture.gr

The Acropolis is the most important ancient site in the Western world. Crowned by the Parthenon, it's visible from almost everywhere in Athens. Its marble gleams white in the midday sun and takes on a honey hue as the sun sinks, then glows above the city by night. A glimpse of this magnificent sight cannot fail to exalt your spirit.

Propylaia

The monumental entrance to the Acropolis, the Propylaia was built by Mnesicles between 437 BCE and 432 BCE, and consists of a central hall with two wings on either side. In ancient times its five gates were the only entrances to the 'upper city'. The middle gate opens onto the Panathenaic Way. The ceiling of the central hall was painted with gold stars on a dark-blue background. The northern wing was used as a *pinakothiki* (art gallery).

Beulé Gate & Monument of Agrippa

Just outside the Propylaia lies the Beulé Gate, named after French archaeologist Ernest Beulé, who uncovered it in 1852. The 8m pedestal halfway up the zigzagging ramp to the Propylaia was once topped by the Monument of Agrippa. This bronze statue of the Roman general riding a chariot was erected in 27 BCE to commemorate victory in the Panathenaic Games.

Temple of Athena Nike

This tiny but exquisitely proportioned Pentelic marble temple was designed by Kallicrates and originally built around 425 BCE; it has been restored three times, most recently in 2003. The internal cella housed a wooden statue of Athena as Victory (Nike), and the exterior friezes illustrated scenes from mythology, the Battle of Plataea (479 BCE) and Athenians fighting Boeotians and Persians. Parts of the frieze are in the Acropolis Museum, as are some relief sculptures, including the beautiful depiction of Athena Nike fastening her sandal.

Parthenon

The Parthenon is the monument that more than any other epitomises the glory of Ancient Greece. It is dedicated to Athena Parthenos, the goddess embodying the power and prestige

★ Top Tips

○ Visit first thing in the morning or late in the day and allow about 1½ hours.

○ The main entrance is from Dionysiou Areopagitou near the Odeon of Herodes Atticus. The east entrance, near the Akropoli metro, can be less crowded.

○ Large bags must be checked, at the main (west) entrance.

○ Wheelchairs access the site via a cage lift; call ahead to arrange (☎ 210 321 4172).

○ Buy the ticket online (www.etickets.tap.gr), or the combo ticket at a smaller tourist site, to avoid the ticket-booth line at the Acropolis.

○ Check http://odysseus.culture.gr for free-admission holidays and changing opening hours.

✕ Take a Break

Swing in to Dionysos Zonar's (p48) for coffee and views of the monument.

Or book ahead for a late-afternoon lunch at Mani Mani (p48).

of the city. One of the largest Doric temples ever completed in Greece, it was designed by Iktinos and Kallicrates to be the pre-eminent monument of the Acropolis and was completed in time for the Great Panathenaic Festival of 438 BCE.

Columns

The Parthenon's fluted Doric columns achieve perfect form. The eight columns at either end and 17 on each side were ingeniously curved to create an optical illusion: the foundations (like all the 'horizontal' surfaces of the temple) are slightly concave and the columns are slightly convex, making both appear straight. Supervised by Pheidias, the sculptors worked on the architectural detail of the Parthenon, including the pediments, frieze and metopes, which were brightly coloured and gilded.

Pediments

The temple's pediments (the triangular elements topping the east and west facades) were filled with elaborately carved three-dimensional sculptures. The west side depicted Athena and Poseidon in their contest for the city's patronage, the east Athena's birth from Zeus' head. See their remnants and the rest of the Acropolis' sculptures and artefacts in the Acropolis Museum (p44).

Metopes & Frieze

The Parthenon's metopes, designed by Pheidias, are square carved panels set between channelled triglyphs. The metopes on the eastern side depicted the Olympian gods fighting the giants, and on the western side

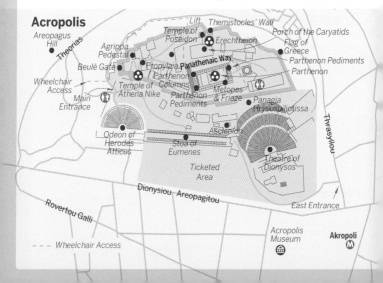

Acropolis

Areopagus Hill
Theorias
Beulé Gate
Agrippa Pedestal
Wheelchair Access
Main Entrance
Temple of Athena Nike
Propylaia
Parthenon Columns
Parthenon Pediments
Temple of Poseidon
Lift
Themistocles' Wall
Erechtheion
Panathenaic Way
Porch of the Caryatids
Flag of Greece
Parthenon Pediments
Parthenon
Metopes & Frieze
Panagia Chrysospiliotissa
Asclepion
Odeon of Herodes Atticus
Stoa of Eumenes
Ticketed Area
Theatre of Dionysos
Thrasyllou
Dionysiou Areopagitou
East Entrance
Rovertou Galli
Acropolis Museum
Akropoli
M
- - - Wheelchair Access

The Acropolis Through History

Contest for Athens

The founding of Athens is enshrined in myth. Phoenician king Kekrops, the story goes, founded a city on a huge rock near the sea. The gods of Olympus proclaimed that it should be named for the deity who could provide the most valuable legacy for mortals. Athena (goddess of wisdom, among other things) produced an olive tree, symbol of peace and prosperity. Poseidon (god of the sea) struck a rock with his trident, creating a saltwater spring, to signify great maritime power (though some versions say he produced a horse). It was a close contest, but the gods judged that Athena's gift, which would provide food, oil and fuel, would better serve the citizens.

Building the Acropolis

The Acropolis was first inhabited in Neolithic times (4000–3000 BCE). The earliest temples were built during the Mycenaean era, in homage to the goddess Athena. People lived on the Acropolis until the late 6th century BCE, but in 510 BCE the Delphic oracle declared it the sole province of the gods. After all the buildings on the Acropolis were reduced to ashes by the Persians on the eve of the Battle of Salamis (480 BCE), Pericles set about his ambitious rebuilding program. He transformed the Acropolis into a city of temples, which has come to be regarded as the zenith of Classical Greece. He spared no expense – only the best materials, architects, sculptors and artists were good enough for a city dedicated to the cult of Athena. It was a showcase of lavishly coloured buildings and gargantuan, painted statues, some of bronze, others of marble plated with gold and encrusted with precious stones.

Preserving the Site

Foreign occupation, inept renovations, visitors' footsteps, earthquakes and, more recently, acid rain and pollution have all taken their toll on the surviving monuments. The worst blow was in 1687, when the Venetians attacked the Turks, opening fire on the Acropolis and causing an explosion in the Parthenon – where the Turks had been storing gunpowder – and damaging all the buildings. And in 1801, Thomas Bruce, Earl of Elgin, spirited away a portion of the Parthenon frieze, which is still on display in the British Museum, despite Greece's ongoing campaign for its return. The Acropolis became a World Heritage site in 1987. Major restoration programs are ongoing. Most of the original sculptures and friezes have been moved to the Acropolis Museum, so what you see now on the hill are replicas.

they showed Theseus leading the Athenian youths into battle against the Amazons.

The southern metopes illustrated the contest of the Lapiths and centaurs at a marriage feast, while the northern ones depicted the sacking of Troy. The internal cella was topped by the Ionic frieze, a continuous sculptured band depicting the Panathenaic Procession.

Statue of Athena Parthenos

The statue for which the temple was built and which once stood at its centre – the Athena Parrthenos (Athena the Virgin) – was considered one of the wonders of the ancient world. It was taken to Constantinople in 426 CE, where it disappeared. Designed by Pheidias and completed in 432 BCE, it stood almost 12m high on its pedestal and was plated in gold. Athena's face, hands and feet were made of ivory, and the eyes fashioned from jewels.

Erechtheion

The Erechtheion, completed around 406 BCE, was a sanctuary built on the most sacred part of the Acropolis: the spot where Poseidon struck the ground with his trident, and where Athena produced the olive tree. Named after Erechtheus, a mythical king of Athens, the temple housed the cults of Athena, Poseidon and Erechtheus. This supreme example of Ionic architecture was ingeniously built on several levels to compensate for the uneven bedrock.

Porch of the Caryatids

The Erechtheion is immediately recognisable by the six majestic maiden columns, the Caryatids (415 BCE), that support its southern portico. Modelled on women from Karyai (modern-day Karyes, in Lakonia), each figure is thought to have held a libation bowl in one hand, and to be drawing up her dress with the other. Those you see are plaster casts. The originals (except for one removed by Lord Elgin, now in the British Museum) are in the Acropolis Museum.

Temple of Poseidon

Poseidon's cella, the Erechtheion's northern porch, is accessible by a small set of stairs against the boundary wall. It consists of six Ionic columns; the fissure in the floor is supposedly left either by Poseidon's trident in his contest with Athena, or by Zeus' thunderbolt when he killed Erechtheus.

Themistocles' Wall

Crafty general Themistocles (524–459 BCE) hastened to build a protective wall around the Acropolis and in so doing incorporated elements from archaic temples on the site. When you're down the hill in Monastiraki, look for the column drums built into the wall on the north side of the Erechtheion.

Odeon of Herodes Atticus

The largest structure on the south slope is a magnificent ancient theatre, the Odeon of Herodes Atticus (p47), built in 161 CE and still in use. The path leads along the top edge; from this vantage the space looks positively intimate, though in fact it seats 5000 people.

Asclepion & Stoa of Eumenes

East of the odeon is the **Asclepion**, a temple built around a sacred spring. The worship of Asclepius, the physician son of Apollo, began in Epidavros and was introduced to Athens in 429 BCE at a time when plague was sweeping the city: people sought cures here.

Beneath the Asclepion, the **Stoa of Eumenes** is a colonnade built by Eumenes II, King of Pergamum (197–159 BCE), as a shelter and promenade for theatre audiences.

Theatre of Dionysos

The 6th-century-BCE timber **theatre** (Dionysiou Areopagitou) that stood here is thought to be

the world's first. Reconstructed in stone and marble between 342 and 326 BCE, the theatre held 17,000 spectators (spread over 64 tiers, of which only about 20 survive) and an altar to Dionysos in the orchestra pit.

Thrones & Carvings

The ringside Pentelic marble thrones were for dignitaries and priests. The grandest, with lions' paws, satyrs and griffins, was reserved for the Priest of Dionysos. The 2nd-century-BCE reliefs at the rear of the stage depict the exploits of Dionysos.

Statues of hefty *selini* stood here too. These were worshippers of the mythical Selinos, the debauched father of the satyrs, whose favourite pastime was charging up mountains with his oversized phallus in lecherous pursuit of nymphs. The *selini* are in a sheltered area near the ticket booth for protection from the weather.

The Odeon of Herodes Atticus

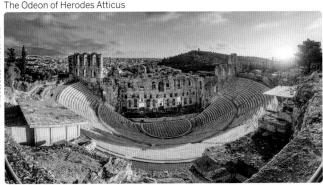

F11PHOTO/SHUTTERSTOCK ©

Top Experience

Examine Treasures at the Acropolis Museum

The state-of-the-art Acropolis Museum displays treasures from the temple hill, with emphasis on the Acropolis as it was in the 5th century BCE, the apotheosis of Greece's artistic achievement. Layers of history are revealed; glass floors expose subterranean ruins, and the Acropolis itself is visible through the floor-to-ceiling windows, so the masterpieces are always in context.

◎ MAP P46, C3

www.theacropolismu
seum.gr

Foyer Gallery

Finds from the slopes of the Acropolis fill the entry, where the floor's slope echoes the climb up the sacred hill. Glass reveals the ruins beneath the museum foundation. Objects here include votive offerings from sanctuaries and, near the entrance, two clay statues of Nike.

Archaic Gallery

The 1st floor is a veritable forest of statues, including some stunning 6th-century *kore* (maiden) statues: young women in draped clothing and elaborate braids. Most were recovered from a pit on the Acropolis, where the Athenians buried them after the Battle of Salamis. The youth bearing a calf, from 570 BCE, is one of the rare male statues discovered.

Early Temple Treasures

The Archaic Gallery also houses bronze figurines and interesting finds from temples predating the Parthenon. These include elaborate pedimental sculptures of Heracles slaying the Lernaean Hydra and a lioness devouring a bull.

Caryatids

On the mezzanine of the 1st floor are the five grand Caryatids, the world-famous maiden columns that held up the porch of the Erechtheion. (The sixth is in the British Museum.)

Parthenon Gallery

The museum's crowning glory, the top-floor glass atrium showcases the Parthenon's pediments, metopes and 160m frieze. When the museum opened in 2007, it marked the first time in more than 200 years that the frieze was displayed in sequence, depicting the full Panathenaic Procession. In between golden-hued originals are white plaster replicas of missing pieces – the controversial Parthenon Marbles taken to Britain by Lord Elgin in 1801.

★ **Top Tips**

● Buy tickets online to skip the queue.

● EU students and under-18s enter free; non-EU students, youth, and people with some disabilities, plus EU citizens over 65, get reduced admission. Bring ID.

● Leave time for the fine museum shop (ground floor) and the film describing the history of the Acropolis (top floor).

● Last admission is 30 minutes before closing, and galleries are cleared 15 minutes before closing, starting at the top.

● You can visit the restaurant on the top floor without paying; ask at the desk.

✕ **Take a Break**

The museum's **cafe-restaurant** on the 2nd floor has superb views and surprisingly reasonable prices (mains €14 to €17). Eat inside or sip a coffee alfresco on the terrace. If you want cheaper eats, head for Mikro Politiko (p49) for souvlaki.

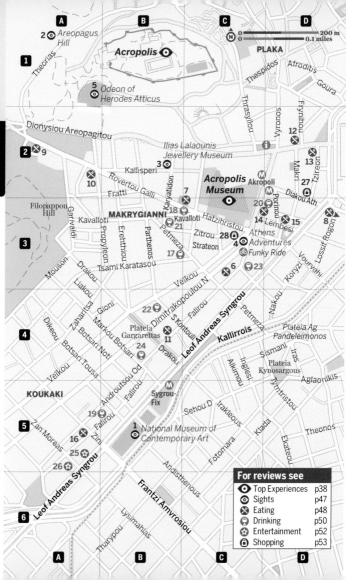

Acropolis Area

A **B** **C** **D**

1

2 Areopagus Hill

Acropolis

Theorias

PLAKA

Thespidos

Afroditis

Goura

5 Odeon of Herodes Atticus

Dionysiou Areopagitou

Ilias Lalaounis Jewellery Museum

Thrasyllou

Fryníhou

Vyronos

12

2

9

Kallisperi

3

Acropolis Museum

Akropoli

Makri

Tziréon

13

27

10

Rovertou Galli

Fratti

Karyatidon

7

Diakou Ath

Filopappou Hill

Garivaldi

MAKRYGIANNI

18

Kavalloti

Hatzihristou

Portinou

20

14 Lembesi

15

8

Kavalloti

Propyleon

Erehthiou

Partheros

21

Zitrou

28

Athens Adventures

Lossif Rogon

Vourvahi

Mouson

Drakou

Tsami Karatasou

17

Stateon

4

Funky Ride

Koryzi

Nakou

3

Liakou

Gioni

Veikou

6

23

Petmeza

4

Drakou

Zaharitsa

Markou Botsari

22

Dimitrakopoulou N

S Kontouli

Falirou

Leof Andreas Syngrou

Kallirrois

Plateia Ag Pandeleimonos

Dikeou

Botsari Noti

Plateia Gargarettas

11

24

Drakou

Sismani

Iras

Plateia Kynosargous

Inglesi

Alkimou

Tzyrtristou

Aglaonikis

5

KOUKAKI

Veikou

Botsari Tousa

Androutsou Od

Falirou

Sygrou-Fix

Sehou D

Irakleous

Fotomara

Klada

Ekateou

Theonos

Zan Moreas

16

19

Falirou

Zini

1 National Museum of Contemporary Art

Andisthenous

25

26

Leof Andreas Syngrou

Frantzi Amvrosiou

Lysimahias

Tharypou

For reviews see	
💠 Top Experiences	p38
💠 Sights	p47
💠 Eating	p48
💠 Drinking	p50
💠 Entertainment	p52
💠 Shopping	p53

A **B** **C** **D**

0 — 200 m
0 — 0.1 miles

Sights

National Museum of Contemporary Art

MUSEUM

1 MAP P46, B5

Set in the former Fix Brewery, this contemporary museum emerged in 2020 from extensive renovations with state-of-the-art galleries for displaying rotating exhibitions of Greek and international art in all media, from painting to video to experimental architecture. (www.emst.gr)

Areopagus Hill

PARK

2 MAP P46, A1

This rocky outcrop below the Acropolis (p38) has great views over the Ancient Agora (p58). According to mythology, it was here that Ares was tried by the council of the gods for the murder of Halirrhothios, son of Poseidon.

The council accepted his defence of justifiable homicide on the grounds that he was protecting his daughter, Alcippe, from unwanted advances.

Ilias Lalaounis Jewellery Museum

MUSEUM

3 MAP P46, B2

A museum for fashionistas: Ilias Lalaounis adorned Elizabeth Taylor and Melina Mercouri, among many others, and is responsible for a singularly Greek style of bold, classically inspired gold jewellery.

This museum showcases a selection from a collection of 4500 pieces, which draws on everything from Greek wildflowers to pre-Columbian motifs. (www.lalaounisjewelrymuseum.gr)

Athens Adventures

TOURS

4 MAP P46, C3

Run by the team at Athens Backpackers, this group offers a very popular Athens walking tour (€7; 10am Monday to Saturday), departing from Athens Sports Bar. (www.athensadventures.gr)

Odeon of Herodes Atticus

THEATRE

5 MAP P46, A1

This amphitheatre was built in 161 CE by wealthy Roman Herodes Atticus in memory of his wife Regilla. It was excavated in 1857–58 and restored in the 1950s.

Capture the Flag

The one modern detail on the Acropolis (aside from the ever-present scaffolding and cranes) is the large Greek flag at the far east end. In 1941, early in the Nazi occupation, two teenage boys climbed up the cliff and raised the Greek flag; their act of resistance is commemorated on a brass plaque nearby.

Easy Riding

Riding a rental bike around the Acropolis area is a good way to see the sights and catch a breeze: try **Funky Ride** (Map p46, C3; www.funkyride.gr). Or since Athens can be hilly, rent an electric bike from **Solebike** (p22). It also offers guided tours available in English, French, Italian and Spanish.

Eating

Mani Mani
GREEK €€

6 MAP P46, C3

Head upstairs to the relaxing, elegant dining rooms of this delightful modern restaurant, which specialises in herb-filled cuisine from the Mani region in the Peloponnese. Standouts include the chicken stuffed with mushrooms and pecorino cheese and seafood orzo with wild fennel. (www.manimani.com.gr)

Point-a
MEDITERRANEAN €€€

7 MAP P46, C3

The rooftop restaurant of the Herodion Hotel, with stunning Acropolis and Acropolis Museum views, serves guests and locals alike. Signature 'tapas cocktails' are served with a savoury appetiser, such as honey-topped *loukoumadhes* (doughnuts) filled with Elassona *manouri* cheese.

Dishes are a creative presentation of traditional Greek specialities. (www.acropolispoint.com;)

Veganaki
VEGAN €

8 MAP P46

A fine addition to Athens' vegan dining options, this convivial spot may overlook a busy road, but inside all is calm as customers enjoy falafel wraps and plates, sandwiches and traditional Greek pies, some of which are also gluten free. Also served here, a great cup of fair-trade organic coffee. (www.facebook.com/VeganakiGR)

Dionysos Zonar's
MEDITERRANEAN €€€

9 MAP P46, A2

Directly across from the Acropolis main entrance, this is ground zero for tour-bus lunches. But you could do a lot worse if you're in need of a restorative coffee; in the evening, when the big groups move out, upper-level tables have a clear view of the south slope of the Acropolis. Food is pricey but good, and service is attentive. (www.dionysoszonars.gr)

Strofi
GREEK €€

10 MAP P46, A2

Book ahead for a Parthenon view from the rooftop of this exquisitely renovated town house. Food is simple grilled meats and fish, but the setting, with elegant white linen and excellent service, elevates the experience to romantic levels. (www.strofi.gr)

Peas

VEGAN €

11 MAP P46, B4

With the sub-name 'Vegan & Raw', this tiny, cheery storefront is an oasis for those seeking alternatives to the animal-based aspects of Greek food. Your chance for seitan or mushroom souvlaki, veggie burgers and bodacious salads, or raw treats like zucchini noodles with herbs and cashew 'Parmesan'. (www.peas.gr)

Mikro Politiko

FAST FOOD €

12 MAP P46, D2

Just the thing to stave off post-Acropolis collapse: a quick souvlaki or falafel from this little place. It's markedly better than other snack options in the area, with fresh ingredients and good salads too. There are benches out front, or the pleasant staff can pack food to go.

Fresko Yogurt Bar

DESSERTS €

13 MAP P46, D2

Delicious Greek yoghurt is the base of all things here. Either fresh or in smoothie form, you can pair it with any number of toppings, from chocolate to black-cherry spoon sweets. A perfect cool-off after seeing the Acropolis. (www.freskoyogurtbar.gr)

Greek Stories

GREEK €€

14 MAP P46, C3

In the swamp of tourist traps across from the Acropolis Museum, Greek Stories stands out for creative takes on Greek staples. The welcome is warm and the people-watching can't be beaten. (www.facebook.com/greekstoriesrestaurant)

Aglio, Olio & Peperoncino

ITALIAN €€

15 MAP P46, D3

The food at this cosy Italian trattoria is simple pastas and the like, satisfying and reasonably priced. It's enhanced by the pleasure of finding this place on a quiet side street and evading the restaurant touts facing the nearby Acropolis Museum. Closed August. (www.facebook.com/lapastadiiraklis)

Fabrika tou Efrosinou

GREEK €€

16 MAP P46, A5

Named for the patron saint of cooks, this 'factory' is really a two-level restaurant focusing on good

Local Restaurant Row

Drakou between Veïkou and Leoforos Syngrou is a tree-shaded pedestrian street dotted with bars and cafes. While no single place excels, it's a good destination when you just want to be out of the tourist fray.

Combined Entrance Tickets

Archaeological sites A €30 combo ticket covers entry to the following:

o **Acropolis** (p38)

o **Ancient Agora** (p58)

o **Roman Agora** (p66)

o **Hadrian's Library** (p67)

o **Kerameikos** (p158)

o **Temple of Olympian Zeus** (p118)

o **Aristotle's Lyceum** (p109) The ticket is valid for five days and can be purchased at any of the included sites or online.

Museums A €15 ticket, valid for three days, covers the following museums:

o **National Archaeological Museum** (p130)

o **Byzantine & Christian Museum** (p108)

o **Epigraphical Museum** (p137)

o **Numismatic Museum** (p108)

ingredients and rarer Greek recipes. When everything is swinging, it's the perfect combination of bountiful, healthy food, including organic vegetables and farmstead cheeses, excellent Greek wines and atmosphere. (www.fabricaefrosinou.gr)

Drinking

Lotte Cafe-Bistrot

CAFE

17 🚇 MAP P46, B3

Hide away from central Athens' noise at this small, just-this-side-of-twee cafe. Sit outside in a private-feeling patch of tree-covered sidewalk, or inside among vintage books and tea sets. Food is homemade cakes and light snacks (€4 to €7). (🕿)

Little Tree Book Cafe

CAFE

18 🚇 MAP P46, C3

This friendly social hub is much beloved by neighbourhood residents, who go for books (they stock a small selection of translated Greek authors here), but also excellent coffee, cocktails and snacks. (www.facebook.com/littletreebooksandcoffee)

Materia Prima

WINE BAR

19 MAP P46, B5

Forget your typical image of a wine bar: Materia Prima is all light and air and blonde wood, with an admirable dedication to artisan winemaking in Greece and beyond. (www.materiaprima.gr)

Hitchcocktales

COCKTAIL BAR

20 MAP P46, D3

Images from Alfred Hitchcock movies are spray-painted on the wall in front of this bar on a quiet street with pillows out front for lounging. The bartenders are polished, and the soundtrack is usually lively swing, jazz, soul and funk. The noise level in the industrial-look raw-concrete space can spike later in the night. (www.facebook.com/hitchcock.athens)

Drupes & Drips

CAFE

21 MAP P46, B3

A coffee to speed your step up to the Acropolis in the morning, or an Aperol spritz or glass of wine to soothe you into the evening on the way down – that's what this pocket-sized cafe/wine bar is all about. Pair your drink with a small plate of something, usually involving the bread from Takis Bakery across the way. (www.facebook.com/drupesdrips)

The Temple of Nike

AERIAL-MOTION/SHUTTERSTOCK ©

Sfika
BAR

22 MAP P46, B4

Glowing yellow inside (perhaps for its namesake; *sfika* means 'wasp'), this small neighbourhood cafe-restaurant-bar has an alternative/student vibe and occasional live music. (www.facebook.com/sfikapub)

Tiki Athens
BAR

23 MAP P46, C3

Kitschy bachelor-pad decor, an Asian-inspired menu and an alternative young crowd make this two-storey spot a fun place for a drink. There's usually live music on Wednesday and Thursday. (www.tikiathens.com)

Ancient Promenade

You could skip all the sights in Athens and still feel you've gotten the city's pulse just by strolling along the pedestrian street of Dionysiou Areopagitou around sundown. Lights glow on the Acropolis above, and the road is filled with tourists, snack vendors, musicians and local couples out for an arm-in-arm promenade. At the intersection with Parthenos, note the outline of a building foundation – it marks the remains of a Roman villa now covered by the street.

Duende
BAR

With the golden glow of a Parisian brasserie, this intimate pub (see 13 MAP p46, D2), is a good place for a grown-up glass of wine or whisky (though not so much for food or cocktails). It's especially welcome as a respite from the tourist bustle nearby. Closed in summer. (www.facebook.com/DuendeAthens)

Kinono
CAFE

24 MAP P46, B4

This two-level cafe-bar has a contemporary style; all blonde wood and industrial fittings, softened with plants and homey touches. It's a popular hang-out for coffees and cocktails and is one of several good cafes all in a row.

Entertainment

Mikrokosmos
CINEMA

25 MAP P46, A5

Why leave all the film fun to the outdoor cinemas? This art-house theatre has comfy plush seats and a bar. (www.mikrokosmoscinema.gr)

Koukles
LIVE PERFORMANCE

26 MAP P46, A5

Come to this long-running club for a kitschy, glam drag show that usually doesn't kick off until at least 1am. (www.facebook.com/Kouklesclubathens)

Athens: Birthplace of Theatre

The Festival of the Great Dionysia

The tyrant Peisistratos introduced the annual Festival of the Great Dionysia during the 6th century BCE, and held it in the world's first theatre, on the south slope of the Acropolis. Masses of people attended the contests, where men clad in goatskins sang and danced, followed by feasting and revelry. Drama as we know it dates to these contests. At one of them, Thespis left the ensemble and took centre stage for a solo performance, an act considered to be the first true dramatic performance – hence the term 'thespian'.

Drama in the Golden Age

During the golden age in the 5th century BCE, the annual festival was one of the state's major events. Politicians sponsored dramas by writers such as Aeschylus, Sophocles and Euripides, with some light relief provided by the bawdy comedies of Aristophanes. People came from all over Attica, with their expenses met by the state.

Greek Theatre Today

Athens continues to support an excellent theatre scene. The works of the classical Greek playwrights are still performed regularly, most notably during the summer **Athens Epidaurus Festival** (p22), which stages the classics (and more contemporary works) at the **Odeon of Herodes Atticus** (p47) and the stunningly preserved theatre in Epidavros in the Peloponnese.

In winter, Athens' 200-plus theatres present everything from Sophocles to Beckett to works by contemporary Greek playwrights. The **National Theatre** (p143) and the **Megaron** (p19) are the best places to catch shows with English surtitles.

Shopping

Melissinos Art

SHOES

27 ⬛ MAP P46, D2

Pantelis Melissinos continues the sandal-making tradition started by his grandfather in 1920 and made famous by his poet/cobbler father Stavros, who built his reputation crafting classical-inspired shoe designs for Hollywood stars and VIPs. (www.melissinos-art.com)

Lovecuts

CLOTHING

28 ⬛ MAP P46, C3

Greek designer Maria Panagiotou makes all the cute, affordable cotton clothing here, such as reversible hoodies, skirts and blouses in fun prints. (www.lovecuts.gr)

Walking Tour 🥾

Ancient Athens

The key ancient sites of Athens make for an action-packed but manageable walk, from the Temple of Olympian Zeus, past the Acropolis Museum and up to the Acropolis, then down around the other side of the hallowed hill into the Plaka and Monastiraki neighbourhoods, where you will find the Ancient Agora and Roman Agora. If you have only one day to see the sights, this is the walk to take.

Walk Facts

Start Temple of Olympian Zeus; metro Akropoli

Finish Ancient Agora; metro Monastiraki, Thissio

Length 2.4km; 3.5 hours

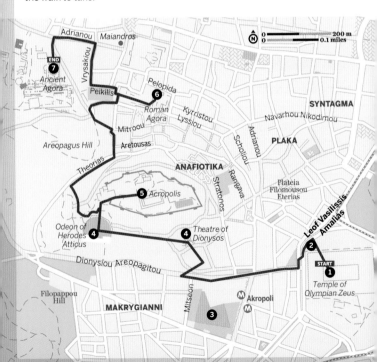

❶ Temple of Olympian Zeus

The striking Temple of Olympian Zeus (p118), the largest temple in Greece, had 104 Corinthian columns, of which 15 remain. Construction began in the 6th century BCE, and Hadrian finally completed it in 131 CE.

❷ Hadrian's Arch

Teetering on the edge of traffic, Hadrian's Arch is the ornate gateway erected in 132 CE to mark the boundary between Hadrian's new monuments and the ancient city.

❸ Acropolis Museum

The landmark Acropolis Museum (p44) displays the precious sculptures from the Acropolis. These include the caryatids and amazing works from the Parthenon's pediments, metopes and frieze.

❹ Ancient Theatres

Enter the Acropolis area via the eastern gate and, on the way up the southern slope of the Acropolis, explore the **Theatre of Dionysos** (p43) – the birthplace of theatre – and the magnificent **Odeon of Herodes Atticus** (p42, p47).

❺ Acropolis

The Acropolis (p38) is the most important ancient site in the Western world. Take in its diminutive, restored Temple of Athena Nike, then enter through the grand gates of the Propylaia to visit the iconic Parthenon as well as the Erechtheion, edged with caryatids, the embodiment of 'statuesque'. On a clear day you can see for miles from the hilltop.

❻ Roman Agora

Exit the Acropolis from the west gate and walk down to Athens' 2nd-century commercial centre: the Roman Agora (p66). The highlight is the well-preserved **Tower of the Winds** (p66). Built in the 1st century BCE, it functioned as an ingenious sundial, weather vane and water clock.

❼ Ancient Agora

The Ancient Agora (p58) was the seat of democracy, philosophy and commerce. This rambling site, with the superb **Temple of Hephaistos**, also has a top-notch museum in the colonnaded Stoa of Attalos.

✕ Take a Break

Two of the easiest spots to stop are the Acropolis Museum's restaurant, with its magical views of the Parthenon, and **Maiandros** (p70), among the many options on Adrianou near the Ancient Agora, for traditional Greek snacks.

Explore ◈
Monastiraki
& Psyrri

Monastiraki's busy square is one of Athens' key hubs, where people meet before hitting nearby bars and souvlaki joints. To the south, the fascinating Ancient Agora (p58) was the city's original civic meeting place. And to the north and west, creatively graffiti-ed Psyrri may look dilapidated, but it's one of the city's liveliest quarters, where restaurants and bars coexist with workshops.

The Short List

○ **Temple of Hephaistos (p60)** *Posing for a pic in front of Greece's best-preserved temple, inside the Ancient Agora, the centre of classical Greek life.*

○ **Tower of the Winds (p66)** *Marvelling at the ancient ingenuity of this octagonal building, which used to function as a time-and-weather centre. Now its beautiful relief carvings are the draw.*

○ **Local art (p77)** *Checking out what's showing at A.antonopoulou.art, one of several galleries in an area that is also liberally covered with giant street art.*

○ **Souvlaki (p69)** *Savouring Athens' meat-on-a-stick tradition at perennial favourite, Kostas, on Plateia Agia Irini.*

Getting There & Around

Ⓜ Monastiraki station (blue and green lines) is the most central stop.

Ⓜ Thissio (green line) is also convenient for Psyrri.

Ⓜ Omonia (green and red lines) is closest to the central market and the north part of Psyrri.

Monastiraki & Psyrri Map on p64

View of Acropolis from Monastiraki MILAN GONDA/SHUTTERSTOCK ©

Top Experience 📷
Step into the Past at the Ancient Agora

⊙ MAP P64, D5

http://odysseus.culture.gr

Starting in the 6th century BCE, this area was Athens' commercial, political and social hub. Socrates expounded his philosophy here, and St Paul preached here. The site today has been cleared of later Ottoman buildings to reveal only classical remains. It's a green respite, with a well-restored temple, a good museum and a Byzantine church.

Stoa of Attalos

In architectural terms, a stoa is a covered portico, but the ancient model, this stoa built by King Attalos II of Pergamum (159–138 BCE), was essentially an ancient shopping mall. The majestic two-storey structure, with an open-front ground floor supported by 45 Doric columns, was filled with storefronts. Today, Greek still uses the word *stoa* for a shopping arcade. The building, which was restored in the 1950s, holds the site museum.

Agora Museum

Packed with archaeological finds, this museum can get uncomfortably crowded if a tour group is cycling through, so time your entrance. You'll find some beautiful sculpture (look for the bronze head of Nike, with inlaid eyes) and superb relics that illustrate how the Agora was used on a daily basis: ancient stone voting machines, coins, terracotta figurines and more. Some of the oldest finds date from 4000 BCE.

Ostraka

On display among the ephemera of daily life are *ostraka* (pottery shards marked with names). These were the 'ballots' by which troublesome citizens were voted out of Athens for a period of 10 years – hence the word 'ostracised'. Many shards here bear the name of Themistocles, a successful 5th-century-BCE ruler whose ambition eventually got him ousted. And one is marked 'Pericles', showing that the leader who created the Athenian empire was not immune from criticism (though he never received enough votes to be ostracised).

Temple of Hephaistos

On the opposite (west) end of the Agora site stands the best-preserved Doric temple in Greece. Built in 449 BCE by Iktinos, one of the architects of the Parthenon, it was dedicated to

★ Top Tips

○ The main (and most reliable) entrance is on Adrianou; the south entrance is open only at peak times.

○ The Temple of Hephaistos is a key photo op: it's well preserved, and you can get quite close.

○ Site clearing starts 30 minutes before closing. Later, visit the Temple of Hephaistos and the Stoa of Attalos, then more central spots.

○ If you're interested in birds, come early: the many trees here harbour a lot of life.

○ Hours change. Check online or call ahead to check.

✕ Take a Break

The site of the Agora is itself a nice break from congested streets. Visit the touristy cafes and restaurants on Adrianou, such as Kuzina (p70), which is a fine lunch spot. Spread across a key corner location on Adrianou, Dioskouri (p73) is good for drinks.

the god of the forge and surrounded by foundries and metalwork shops. It has 34 columns and a frieze on the eastern side depicting nine of the Twelve Labours of Hercules. In 1300 CE it was converted into the Church of Agios Georgios, then deconsecrated in 1934. In 1922 and 1923 it was a shelter for refugees from Asia Minor; iconic photos from that period show families hanging laundry among the pillars and white tents erected along the temple's base.

Stoa Foundations

Northeast of the Temple of Hephaistos are the foundations of the **Stoa of Zeus Eleutherios**, one of the places where Socrates spoke. Further north are the foundations of the **Stoa of Basileios**, as well as the **Stoa Poikile**, or 'Painted Stoa', for its murals of battles of myth and history, rendered by the leading artists of the day.

Council House & Tholos

Southeast of the Temple of Hephaistos, archaeologists uncovered the **New Bouleuterion** (Council House), where the Senate (originally created by Solon) met, while the heads of government met to the south at the circular **Tholos**.

Church of the Holy Apostles

This charming little Byzantine church, near the southern site gate, was built in the 11th century to commemorate St Paul's teaching in the *agora*. Following the style of the

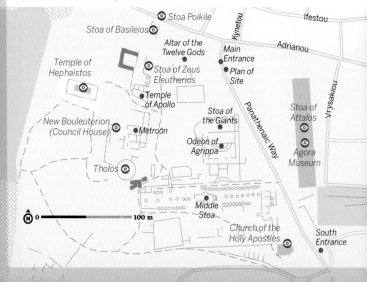

The Great Panathenaic Festival

The biggest event in ancient Athens was the Panathenaic Procession, the climax of the Panathenaic Festival held to venerate the goddess Athena. The route cut through the whole city, including the Ancient Agora. Scenes of the procession are vividly depicted in the 160m-long Parthenon frieze in the Acropolis Museum (p44).

The Contests

There were actually two festivals: a relatively sedate annual one to mark Athena's birthdate, approximately in July, and a grander one every fourth year. This Great Panathenaic Festival began with dancing, followed by athletic, dramatic and musical contests. Starting in the 4th century BCE, the Panathenaic Stadium (p122) hosted many of the athletic events, which included a pentathlon (footracing, discus and javelin throwing, long jump and wrestling), chariot races and the free-fighting match called *pankration*.

Winners were presented with amphorae (vase-shaped ceramic vessels) containing oil from Athens' sacred olive trees; some of these are on display in the National Archaeological Museum (p130).

The Panathenaic Procession

On the final day of the festival, the Panathenaic Procession began at the Dipylon Gate of Kerameikos (p158), led by men carrying animals sacrificed to Athena, followed by maidens carrying *rhytons* (horn-shaped drinking vessels) and musicians playing a fanfare for the girls of noble birth who held aloft the sacred *peplos* (a glorious saffron-coloured shawl). During the preceding year, this select group of young women wove the *peplos* for the festival – a great honour.

The parade followed the Panathenaic Way, which cuts across the Ancient Agora and the middle of the Acropolis. Not everyone was allowed to enter the Acropolis, but in the festival's grand finale, the favoured few ultimately placed the *peplos* on the statue of Athena Polias in the Erechtheion.

time, its external brick decorations mimic Arabic calligraphy. During the period of Ottoman rule, it underwent many changes, but between 1954 and 1957 it was stripped of its 19th-century additions and restored to its original form. It contains several fine Byzantine frescoes, which were transferred from a demolished church.

Walking Tour 🚶

Browsing in the Heart of Monastiraki & Psyrri

Emerging at Monastiraki station, you step right into Athens' vibrant character – the Acropolis above, souvlaki aromas wafting from Mitropoleos, fruit vendors hawking the best of the season and pedestrian lanes lined with enticing shops. If you can, come on a Sunday morning for the flea market, and stay into the afternoon for mezedhes and music at local cafes.

Walk Facts

Start Plateia Avyssinias

End Protogenous at Athinas

Length 1km; one hour

❶ Monastiraki Flea Market

Ifestou is signed as the 'Athens flea market', but it's mostly souvenir shops. The true flea feel is on **Plateia Avyssinias**, where dusty *palaiopoleia* ('old-stuff sellers') rule. The best rummaging is on Sundays, when additional vendors lay out wares along Astingos and other nearby blocks.

❷ One-Stop Shopping

A few popular multiuse spaces in Psyrri and Monastiraki merge gallery, cafe and bar. One popular place is **TAF** (p68), a clutch of barely restored 19th-century houses, with a garden courtyard for drinks, plus an excellent high-design souvenir shop.

❸ Pallados & Protogenous Streets

These eclectic shopping streets mix traditional (rope dealers, handmade baskets) and contemporary goods, as at cool basement shop **Color Skates** (www.colorskates.com), where Athenians get their decks, and **The Real Intellectuals** (www.therealintellectuals.com), home to cool-cat retro motorcycle gear.

❹ Drink Break

For a wee dram or a coffee-based pick-me-up, stop off at **Juan Rodriguez Bar** (www.facebook.com/juanrodriguezbar), especially cosy in winter when you sidle up to the bar in the ornate interior. In summer, people-watch at the few tables set up across the street among the plastic- and tin-ware sellers.

❺ Equestrian Crafts

Of all of Psyrri's niche old shopping districts, the donkey-decoration district might be the niche-est. At tiny **Chrisanthos**, shop for beaded bridles and shepherd bells – or, if you don't have a donkey, a set of worry beads. Just around the corner, chic **Mompso** (https://mompso.com) is the upscale version, catering to Athens' horsey set.

❻ Top Souvlaki

When you get hungry, stroll down to pretty Plateia Agia Irini, to tiny **Kostas** (p69) and its excellent pork souvlaki. A lovely veg-friendly option a couple of blocks north is **Feyrouz** (www.feyrouz.gr; 📷), which does a delicious meatless *lahmajoun* (flatbread topped with spicy paste and filled with vegetables).

❼ A Sweet Finish

Backtrack for dessert at **Kokkion** (www.kokkion.com), a tiny ice-cream shop that does intense fruit flavours (ginger-mandarin, say) and traditional mastic-flavoured *kaimaki* ice cream. There's also a full coffee operation, for an afternoon pick-me-up.

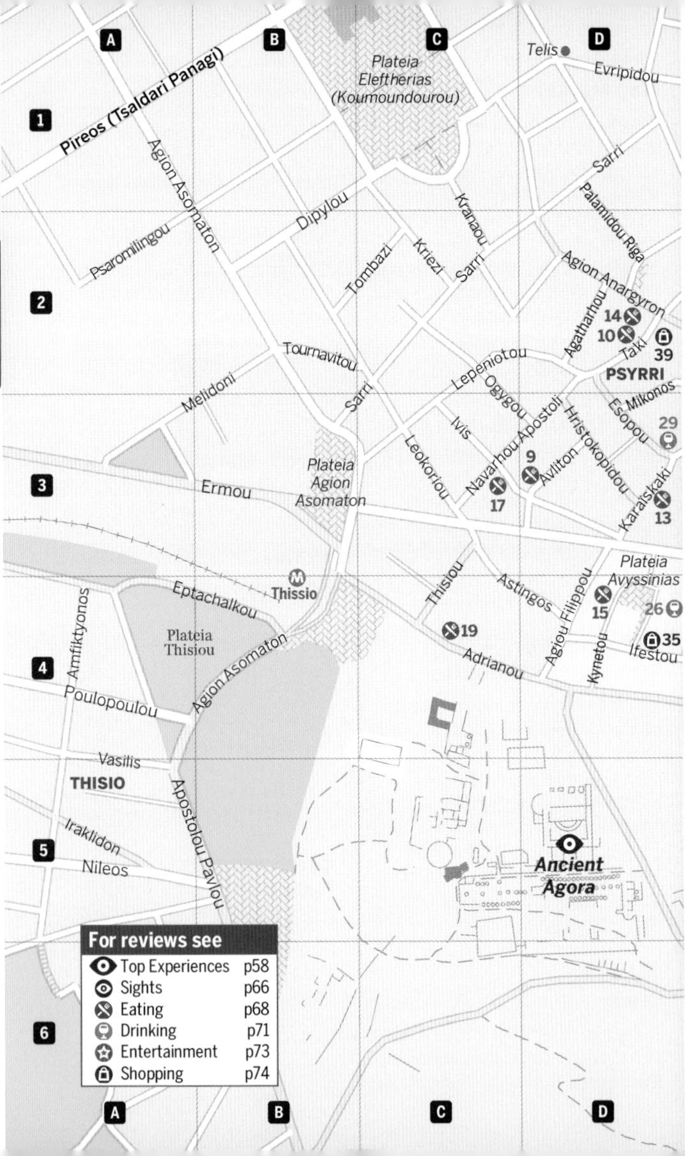

Monastiraki & Psyrri

A
B
C
D

Telis

Evripidou

1

Pireos (Tsaldari Panagi)

Plateia
Eleftherias
(Koumoundourou)

Agion Asomaton

Dipylou

Sarri

Psaromilingou

Kranaou

Tombazi

Palamidou Riga

2

Krezi

Sarri

Agion Anargyron

Agatharhou

14

10
Taxi
39

Tournavitou

Lepeniotou

PSYRRI

Melidoni

Sarri

Ivis

Oxygou

Mikonos

Navarhou Apostoli

Hristokopidou

Esopou

29

Plateia
Agion
Asomaton

Leokoriou

9

Avliton

Ermou

17

Karaiskaki

13

3

Thissio

Thisiou

Astingos

Plateia
Avyssinias

Amfiktyonos

Eptachalkou

15

26

4

Plateia
Thisiou

Agion Asomaton

19

Agiou Filippou

Kynetou

35

Ifestou

Poulopoulou

Adrianou

Vasilis

THISIO

Apostolou Pavlou

5

Iraklidon

Nileos

Ancient
Agora

For reviews see

⊙	Top Experiences	p58
⊙	Sights	p66
✗	Eating	p68
☐	Drinking	p71
✪	Entertainment	p73
⊡	Shopping	p74

6

Aristogitonos

Meat Market

Evripidou

Eolou

Aristidou

Eshylou

Agiou Dimitriou

Aristofanous

Plateia
Iroön

Pallados
Protogenous

Kodrika

Athinas

Athinas

Polyklitou

Vyssis

Voreou

Agathonos

Hrysospiliotissis

Praxitelous

Leoharous

Nikiou

Ag. Markou

Karori

Limbona

Kolokotroni

Miaouli

Thermidos

Avramiotou

Agias Irinis

Skouze

Plateia
Agia Irini

Athinaidos

Klitiou

Romvis

Periklous

Agias Theklas

A for
Athens

Lukumades

Ermou

Couleur
Locale

Plateia
Monastirakiou

City Zen

Church of
Kapnikarea

Normanou

Plateia
Dimopratiriou

Kapnikareas

Plateia
Kapnikareas

Mitropoleos

Athens
Cathedral

Nisou

Monastiraki
MONASTIRAKI

Mosque of
Tzistarakis

Adrianou

Hadrian's
Library

Areos

Pandrosou

Kalogrioni

Plateia Arhaia
Agoras

Plateia
Mitropoleos

Church of Agios
Eleftherios

Vrysakiou

Kladou

Dexippou

Pelopida

Adrianou

Mnisikleous

Vlahou Ang

Agias Filotheis

Peikilis

Epam Inonda

Eolou

Diogenous

PLAKA

Roman
Agora

Tower of
the Winds

Markou Aureliou

Polygnotou

Dioskouron

Panos

Mitroou

Thrasyvoulou

Bath House
of the Winds

Kyrristou

Lyssiou

Flessa

Athens under Roman Rule

A portion of Greece was first taken into the Roman Empire in 146 BCE. In 86 BCE Athens joined an ill-fated rebellion in Asia Minor staged by the king of the Black Sea region, Mithridates VI. In retribution, the Roman statesman Sulla invaded Athens and took off with its most valuable sculptures. As the province of Achaea, the Greek peninsula was officially under the auspices of Rome, but some major cities were granted limited self-rule.

It helped, too, that Romans revered Greek culture, so Athens retained its status as a centre of learning. Under the rule of Roman emperors Augustus, Nero and Hadrian, the city flourished. Hadrian considered the city his empire's cultural capital and invested in a library, temples and an aqueduct. A period of relative peace, the Pax Romana, lasted in Greece until the middle of the 3rd century CE.

Sights

Roman Agora
HISTORIC SITE

 1   MAP P64, E5

This was the city's market area under Roman rule, and it occupied a much larger area than the current site borders. You can see a lot from outside the fence, but it's worth going in for a closer look at the well-preserved **Gate of Athena Archegetis** – financed by Julius Caesar in 10 BCE – the propylaeum (entrance gate) to the market, as well as an Ottoman mosque and the ingenious and beautiful Tower of the Winds, on the east side of the site. (http://odysseus.culture.gr)

Tower of the Winds
MONUMENT

2   MAP P64, F5

This Pentelic marble tower within the Roman Agora, likely built in the 2nd century BCE, is both beautiful and functional. Devised by Andronicus, a Macedonian (Greek) astronomer, it's an ancient time-and-weather station. Aligned with the four cardinal directions, each of its eight sides is a compass point, illustrated with a figure representing the wind from that direction. Sundial markings are visible below the reliefs, and it was topped with a weather vane, probably a bronze figure of Triton.

Inside the tower you can see the original position of a water clock, which marked time with water from a stream that flowed from the Acropolis.

The stone roof, one of very few preserved from ancient times, is 24 stone panels. Conservators have revealed patches of fresco – it was once painted all blue inside. There are also traces of later uses: a faint Roman drawing of a ship, a patch of a Byzantine angel fresco from the time it was used as a church, and Arabic calligraphy and a mihrab (prayer niche) from the late Ottoman period, when Turkish dervishes used it as a *tekke* (a Sufi place of worship).

Hadrian's Library
RUINS

3 ◉ MAP P64, F4

These are the remains of the largest structure erected by Hadrian (2nd century CE). Not just a library, it also held music and lecture rooms. It was laid out as a typical Roman forum, with a pool in the centre of a courtyard bordered by 100 columns. The library's west wall, by the site entrance, has been restored. Beyond are only traces of the library, as well as two churches, built in the 7th and 12th centuries. (http://odysseus.culture.gr)

Athens Cathedral
CHURCH

4 ◉ MAP P64, H5

This ornate 1862 cathedral is the seat of the archbishop of the Greek Orthodox Church of Athens. (http://iaath.gr)

Church of Agios Eleftherios
CHURCH

5 ◉ MAP P64, H5

This 12th-century church, known as the Little Metropolis and dedicated to both Agios Eleftherios and Panagia Gorgoepikoos (Virgin Swift to Hear), is Athens' religious history in one tiny building.

Roman Agora

INU/SHUTTERSTOCK ©

The cruciform-style marble church was erected on the ruins of an ancient temple and its exterior is a mix of medieval beasts and ancient gods in bas-relief, with columns appropriated from older structures.

It was once the city's cathedral, but now stands in the shadows of the much larger new cathedral.

TAF
GALLERY

6 MAP P64, E4

Whether you want a shot of art, a clever design morsel or a refreshing drink, stop in at TAF, a just-barely updated complex of 1870s brick buildings.

The central courtyard is a cafe-bar that fills with an eclectic young crowd, and the surrounding rooms act as galleries, DJ space and an excellent souvenir shop. Events are usually free. (http://theartfoundation. metamatic.gr)

Church of Kapnikarea
CHURCH

7 MAP P64, G4

This small 11th-century church, dedicated to the Virgin Mary, stands smack in the middle of the Ermou shopping strip.

It was saved from the bulldozers and restored by Athens University. Its dome is supported by four large Roman columns.

Most of the interior frescoes were painted by famous artist Fotis Kontoglou in 1955.

Eating

Karamanlidika tou Fani
GREEK €€

8 MAP P64, E1

At this modern-day *pastomage-ireio* (combo tavern-deli) tables are set alongside the deli cases, and staff offer complimentary tasty morsels while you're looking at the menu. Beyond the Greek cheeses and cured meats, there's good seafood, such as marinated anchovies, as well as rarer wines and craft beers. Service is excellent, as is the warm welcome, often from Fani herself. (www. karamanlidika.gr)

Atlantikos
SEAFOOD €€

9 MAP P64, D3

Tucked down a little lane, this small, hip fish restaurant is easy to miss – look for happy people chatting over heaps of shrimp shells. The atmosphere is simple and casual, with low prices to match – but there's excellent-quality seafood, whether it's fried or grilled.

Kalimeres
CAFE €

10 MAP P64, D2

Cheerfully spread across the walking lane with cool tunes floating on the breeze, Kalimeres is a superb low-key spot for brunches and all-day drinks and snacks. (www. kalimeres.gr)

Ottoman Athens

Athens was under Ottoman rule for several centuries, but very few buildings survive, as archaeologists have been more eager to dig up older relics beneath. The largest surviving structure is the **Mosque of Tzistarakis** (Map p64, F4; www.mnep.gr), which has been towering over Plateia Monastirakiou since 1759. The Museum of Greek Folk Art maintains the building, but it has been closed since 2015. The same museum also restored the **Bath House of the Winds** (p87), a typical Ottoman *hammam*.

Just around the corner, the **Roman Agora** (p66) contains a 17th-century mosque (now an exhibit space), and the ancient **Tower of the Winds** (p66) was used by Turkish dervishes as a *tekke* (a Sufi place of worship). Adjoining the *tekke* across the road north of the tower, was a Sufi madrasah, built in the 18th century. In the 19th century, its student cells made it useful as a jail. Much of the building was demolished to excavate Roman ruins beneath. Only the front gate remains, overgrown with greenery.

Kostas

GREEK €

11 MAP P64, G3

On a pleasant square opposite Agia Irini church, this old-style virtual hole-in-the-wall joint grills up tasty souvlaki and *bifteki* (Greek-seasoned hamburger), served on pitta with a spicy tomato sauce. Go before the lunch rush, as it may close early if it runs out of meat.

Luv N Roll

TAPAS €€

13 MAP P64, D3

Are you in the market for a tattoo or piercing or just a delicious small plate with a rooftop Acropolis view? If so, this is the place for you. Flavours skew straight-up Greek and an elaborate cocktail capacity makes it a great all-round experience. (https://luvnroll.com)

EATERY

MEDITERRANEAN €€

12 MAP P64, G3

A welcome break in the bustling commercial district of Monastiraki, EATERY dishes up well-made, fresh Greek and Mediterranean meals. And on a hot day, its frozen cocktails offer a grand pick-me-up. (www.facebook.com/bairaktariseatery)

Nikitas

TAVERNA €

14 MAP P64, D2

Locals swear by this tried-and-true taverna that has been serving reasonably priced, simple and tasty traditional food since well before Psyrri became a hot spot. It's the only place busy on weekdays. Closed August. (www.onikitas.gr)

Hot Grill

A fluorescent-lit beacon of good food and kind service on a grimy block, **Telis** (Map p64, D1) has been serving up simplicity since 1978. There's no menu, just a set meal: a small mountain of charcoal-grilled pork chops atop chips, plus a side vegetable. Greek salad is optional, as is beer or rough house wine.

Café Avissinia
MEZEDHES €€

15 ✗ MAP P64, D4

This antiques-bedecked place on Plateia Avyssinias, in the middle of the antique dealers, has been legendary since the 1980s for its live music and varied mezedhes. It's great for a midday break from the market (p63), or a late supper on a weekend night. In summer, snag Acropolis (p38) views from its terrace. (https://cafeavissinia.net)

Maiandros
GREEK €€

16 ✗ MAP P64, E4

A cut above the array of ho-hum tavernas along Adrianous, Maiandros serves up traditional Greek food in fine form. Staff are friendly but don't push you once you sit down, and there's live bouzouki music. (www.maiandros.eu)

Ivis
MEZEDHES €

17 ✗ MAP P64, C3

This cosy corner place, with its bright arty decor, has a small but delicious range of simple, freshly cooked mezedhes that change daily. A good ouzo and raki selection lights things up.

Bougatsadiko Thessaloniki
PIES €

18 ✗ MAP P64, E2

Unexpected for its location on a key nightlife square in Psyrri, this place makes excellent *pites* (pies), with filo crust that's 'opened' (rolled out by hand) every day – you can watch the baker at work. *Bougatsa* (filo with custard) is great for breakfast, the meat pies are a treat after drinks and *spanakopita* (spinach pie) hits the spot anytime. (www.facebook.com/bougatsadikothessaloniki)

Kuzina
GREEK €€

19 ✗ MAP P64, C4

This comfortably elegant restaurant does chic Greek, with creations such as fried dumplings filled with feta and olives. It's cosy in winter, as light streams in, warming the crowded tables. In summer, book ahead for a rooftop table for views all around. (www.kuzina.gr)

Avli
MEZEDHES €

20 ✗ MAP P64, E1

Cheap, cheerful and borderline chaotic on weekend nights, Avli requires you to squeeze down a narrow hall to get in; you'll wait for service if it's busy. The white-washed walls and outdoor seating give you an island feel, and the *keftedhes* (fried meatballs) and the special omelette, filled with fries and sausage, are excellent drinking food. Closed Tuesdays.

Nancy's Sweethome CAFE €

21 ✖ MAP P64, E2

Get your sugar fix at this place on a bustling square. It's famous for its extra-large cakes swimming in melted chocolate and giant dollops of ice cream. Also has syrup-soaked Greek pastries; a local favourite is the *kunefe,* a sweet cheese pastry served with a generous helping of mastic-flavoured ice cream. Closed August. (www.nancysweethome.gr)

O Thanasis KEBAB €

22 ✖ MAP P64, F4

In the heart of Athens' souvlaki hub, just off Plateia Monastirakiou, O Thanasis is a good place to settle in and watch the street parade. It's known especially for its mince kebabs on pitta. Service can be spotty, though. (www.othanasis.com)

Drinking

Dude Bar BAR

23 🔵 MAP P64, H3

Exceptionally good music – obscure funk and soul that makes you feel like you're living a Quentin Tarantino movie – plays at this

Kokorétsi and lamb grilling over charcoal fire

Snack Bonanza

Stand at the junction of Eolou and Athinaidos and look east and south for a delicious variety of snack food, from fresh falafel to fried fish. Then again, you might not make it past **Lukumades** (Map p64, G3; www.lukumades.com), right on the corner, which serves *loukoumadhes*, Greece's excellent morsels of fried-dough, doused in traditional honey or filled with jam or ice cream.

little bar on a pedestrian street. What's more, the Dude buzzes till practically dawn. (www.facebook. com/thedudebar)

Noel BAR

24 🚇 MAP P64, G3

One of the best of Athens' breed of maximalist-designed cafe-bars, Noel's slogan is 'where it's always Christmas' – meaning the candlelit cocktail-party kind of Christmas, no Santa suits required. Under softly glimmering chandeliers, smartly suited bartenders serve some of the most creative cocktails in town. Music is a mix of 1980s, '90s and jazz. (https://noelbar.gr)

Booze Cooperativa BAR

25 🚇 MAP P64, H3

By day this art mansion is full of young Athenians playing chess

and backgammon and working on their laptops. Later it transforms into a bar that rocks till late. The basement hosts art exhibitions and there's a theatre upstairs. (www.boozecooperativa.com; 📶)

Norman COCKTAIL BAR

26 🚇 MAP P64, D4

Delicious, creative cocktails are the order of the day at this simple storefront on a back alley in Monastiraki. There's not a lot of seating, so have a drink on the go.

Old Fashioned Bar BAR

27 🚇 MAP P64, E3

Chilled out with soul tunes and friendly staff, the Old Fashioned Bar is a reliable staple for cocktails, Guinness on tap and a small bar experience, in the heart of Athens. Sit out on the sidewalk and watch the world go by.

Six d.o.g.s. BAR

28 🚇 MAP P64, F3

The core of this super-creative events space is a rustic, multilevel back garden, a great place for quiet daytime chats over coffee or a relaxed drink. From there, you can head in to one of several adjoining buildings to see a band, art show or other generally cool happening. (https://sixdogs.gr)

Little Kook

CAFE

29 🚇 MAP P64, D3

Nominally, this place sells coffee and cake. But it's really about its dazzling decor, which conjures up childhood fantasies. Precisely which one depends on the season, as the theme changes regularly. Everywhere are dolls, props, paintings and table decorations. You'll know you're getting close when you see party streamers over the street. Kids will be dazzled; Instagrammers will swoon. (www.facebook.com/littlekookgr; 👪)

Tranzistor

BAR

30 🚇 MAP P64, E2

Sidle up to the backlit bar or relax at tables outside at this small, cool spot. It's one of a few good mellow bars on this narrow street. (www.facebook.com/tranzistorcafe)

Orea Hellas

CAFE

31 🚇 MAP P64, F4

This lovely old-style coffee house is a perfect place to take a break from shopping on the Monastiraki strip. Head upstairs for a seat on a balcony overlooking Mitropoleos, or, in cooler weather, an indoor spot with an Acropolis view. Pair your Greek coffee with sweets or a range of solid snacks and salads. Service can be spotty.

Upstairs it also holds the **Center of Hellenic Tradition** crafts shop. (www.facebook.com/OreaHellas; 📶)

Dioskouri

CAFE

32 🚇 MAP P64, E4

This cafe-restaurant sprawls over the road, overlooking the railway line. On the cafe side (Adrianou 39), tables sit under a huge shade tree that gives the place a traditional feel. For coffee, ouzo and snacks, it's popular with students – and of course tourists, thanks to its location on this pedestrian street. Service is uneven, though.

Rooster

LGBTIQ+

33 🚇 MAP P64, G3

This always-busy LGBT+ cafe on lively Plateia Agia Irini is straight-friendly too. The atmosphere is great and it fills up with chatting locals. (www.roostercafe.gr; 📶)

Entertainment

Faust

CABARET

34 ⭐ MAP P64, G3

Loud, raunchy, funny, just plain quirky: eclectic and popular bar Faust hosts it all on its small stage. Some events are free, others ticketed. The place closes from June to August. (www.faust.gr)

Cafe Central

A collection of cafes and bars in Psyrri radiating from Agion Anargyron and Sarri streets make for chill coffee by day and lively cocktails by night.

Shopping

Yiannis Samouelian
MUSICAL INSTRUMENTS

35 🔒 MAP P64, D4

Wedged between more-modern, generic stores on Ifestou, this shop is the place to buy the bouzouki of your dreams; handmade ones cost around €200.

It has been dealing in musical instruments from around the world since 1928. (https://samouelian.gr)

Martinos
ANTIQUES

36 🔒 MAP P64, F4

This Monastiraki landmark opened in 1890 and has an excellent, sometimes museum-quality selection of Greek and European antiques and collectables, including painted dowry chests, icons, coins, glassware, porcelain and furniture. (www.martinosart.gr)

Olgianna Melissinos
SHOES

37 🔒 MAP P64, E4

A scion of the legendary poet/sandalmaker Stavros Melissinos (along with brother Pantelis, who has a separate shop (p53)), Olgianna has a line of custom-fitted sandals as well as smart belts and bags.

She can also make designs to order. (www.melissinos-sandals.gr)

Shedia Home
ARTS & CRAFTS

38 🔒 MAP P64, G3

Meaning 'raft', *Shedia* is Greece's version of street-vendor magazines such as the *Big Issue*.

Unsold copies are now being upcycled into an appealing range of homewares and accessories including papier-mâché lampshades and bowls, earrings and necklaces.

The space beneath its editorial offices has been reimagined as a shop and cafe-bar. (https://shedia-home.gr)

Kartousa
JEWELLERY

39 🔒 MAP P64, D2

Eclectic, folky handmade jewellery and homewares brighten this tiny storefront. (www.kartousa.gr)

Big Bazaar
ANTIQUES

40 🔒 MAP P64, F1

The name of this junk shop is an understatement. Covering two floors, there's room upon room of precariously balanced treasures, so many it's difficult to process, much less pick through. Stash your bags on the ground floor, so you don't knock anything over.

Pan-Pol
HATS

41 🔒 MAP P64, F1

Whether you want a moss-green fedora or a nontouristy Greek fisherman's cap, this shoebox of a shop will have it, along with many other felt hats. Most of the stock comes from a workshop upstairs, and prices start at just €8. (www.panpolhats.gr)

Local Tips for Arts Inspiration

o **Former Public Tobacco Factory** (www.neon.org.gr)

o **Museum of Cycladic Art** (p108)

o **Street art murals in Psyrri and Plaka areas**

o **The Ghika Gallery** (www.benaki.org)

o **Basil & Elise Goulandris Foundation** (p122)

And to find out what's on in Athens, check https://culturei sathens.gr.

Dimitris Fousekis,
local artist,
@dimitris.fousekis

Monastiraki & Psyrri Shopping

Big Bazaar

BALONCICI/SHUTTERSTOCK

Walking Tour 🥾

Wandering the Central Market

The streets around the Athens Central Market (also referred to as the Varvakios Agora) are a sensory delight, all colour and bustle and noisy hawkers' cries. Some of the best, most traditional Athenian food experiences are found here, and you can also feast your eyes on art at some very good galleries nearby.

Walk Facts

Start Athinas, between Sofokleous and Evripidou

End Sarri

Length 1km; one hour

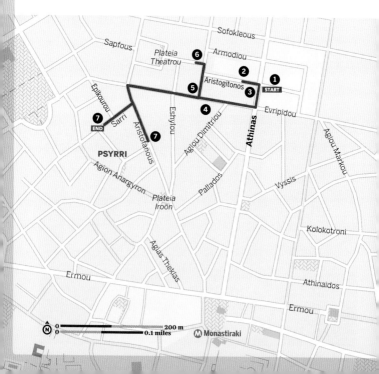

❶ Athens Central Market

A must for gastronomes, the historical **Varvakios Agora** building contains the meat and seafood markets, packed with shiny-eyed fish and ruby-red lamb carcasses. (The vendors have rather famously resisted EU hygiene directives and still display their massive wooden butcher blocks.) For the best energy, come early in the morning or late at night, especially for the 24/7 tavernas.

❷ Fruit & Veg

Across Athinas from the main hall, **produce sellers** set up here every day. The vegetables are lovely to admire, as well as an indicator of what's in peak season – and hence, what to order at restaurants. Surrounding it all are dealers in olives and cheeses, as well as some deeply absorbing junk shops.

❸ Regional Specialities

For a more structured shopping experience, head straight to the **Pantopoleion Kolios**, stocked with traditional products from all over Greece: Santorini capers, Cretan rusks, jars of goodies for edible souvenirs, Greek wines and spirits, plus baked goods and cheeses.

❹ Spice Shops

Along the streets around the market, burlap bags overflow with chillies, dried rosebuds and candied ginger. Wander the shops, enjoying the aromas emanating from within. Try picturesque **Fotsi** (www.fotsi.gr) and the other neighbouring spice shops for a bounty of seasoning.

❺ Meaty Treats

Taste spices in action at **Miran** (www.miran.gr), a local favourite for cured meats, such as *pastourma* (pastrami, but spicier). Or visit **Karamanlidika tou Fani** (www.karamanlidika.gr), a modern-day *pastomageireio* (combo tavern-deli), which offers Greek cheeses and cured meats, as well as good seafood and rarer wines and craft beers. Each has tables to enjoy treats on the spot.

❻ Quirky Taverna

There's no signage at **Diporto Agoras**, one of the dining gems of Athens. Double doors lead to a rustic cellar, where there's no set menu.

The speciality is *revythia* (chickpea stew), followed by grilled fish and washed down with wine from giant barrels. If you're lucky, an accordion player may show up.

❼ Contemporary Art

After lunch, see what's new at two good galleries: **a.antonopoulou. art** (www.aaart.gr) and, just around the corner, **Alibi** (www.alibigallery. com). Excellent street art on these blocks too.

Explore

Syntagma & Plaka

The neighborhood around Plateia Syntagmatos (Syntagma Square), the heart of modern Athens, is all business by day, but after the shops close scores of small bars open. Just a short walk southwest is the heart of old Athens, Plaka, where narrow streets wind by neoclassical mansions and pretty tavernas. It's ground zero for Athens tourism, but still home to lifelong residents.

The Short List

o **Tomb of the Unknown Soldier (p84)** *Getting your prime Athens photo op during the hourly changing of the guard.*

o **Small museums (p85)** *Digging deep at Athens' Jewish Museum; the city's oldest house; a WWII prison and others.*

o **Anafiotika (p86)** *Exploring this tiny corner of Plaka, where Greek island architecture creates a quiet spot below the Acropolis.*

o **National Gardens (p85)** *Wandering in this shady park, and maybe taking in a movie on a summer night in neighbouring Zappeio Gardens.*

Getting There & Around

Ⓜ Syntagma station (blue and red lines) sits at the heart of the city, at Plateia Syntagmatos and a short walk from Plaka.

Ⓜ Monastiraki (blue and green lines) and Akropoli (red line) are also walking distance to Plaka.

Syntagma & Plaka Map on p82

The old Plaka PE DRA/SHUTTERSTOCK ©

Walking Tour 🥾

Quiet Corners of Plaka & Syntagma

Move away from the touristy lowlands of Plaka for a glimpse of old Athens – it's virtually car-free – in narrow lanes winding up the northeastern side of the Acropolis hill, and in the maze of the Anafiotika quarter. Even modern Syntagma shows traces of history when you know where to look.

Walk Facts

Start Mnisikleous, Plaka
End Stadiou, Syntagma
Length 2.4km; two hours

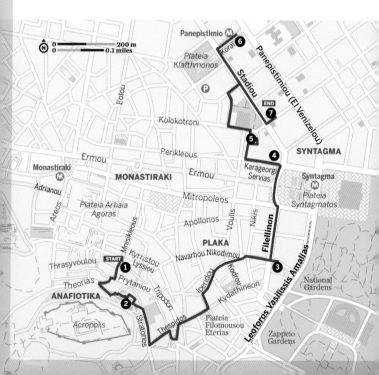

❶ Scenic Staircase

Start out at perhaps the most photogenic street in Plaka, Mnisikleous, where cafes line a long staircase. Neighbourhood residents favour **Yiasemi** (p92) for its vegetarian breakfast buffet and its tempting cakes. Pull up a pillow and perch on the stairs – you're part of the postcard now.

❷ An Island in the City

Further uphill, the tiny **Anafiotika** (p86) area grew in the mid-1800s, when builders from Anafi mimicked their home-island architecture, all whitewash and geraniums. Look for Theorias, a very small street up from Pritaniou. Zigzagging back down the southeast side via Stratonos, you'll pass a surprise **olive grove/local park**.

❸ Byzantine Church

The 1031 **Church of Sotira Lykodimou** (p86) is open more regularly than other old churches here, and it's the largest medieval structure in Athens. It has served as the Russian Orthodox Church since 1847, when Nikiforos Lytras, later famed for his portraiture, was hired out of the School of Fine Arts to paint the uncannily realistic icons.

❹ Rarefied Escape

You don't need to stay in the most prestigious hotel in Athens to enjoy its old-world grandeur. Built in 1862 to accommodate visiting heads of state, the **Grande Bretagne** (www.marriott.com; P ❄ @ 🕿 ⛵), right on Plateia Syntagmatos, offers serene havens from the busy city centre: from high tea in its Winter Garden to rooftop refreshments in its Acropolis-view restaurant and bar.

❺ Coffee & Chocolate Fix

Downtown's shopping arcades yield treasures like premium coffee shop tiny **Kaya**. For dessert, stop at **Aristokratikon** (www. aristokratikon.com), which has been making fine chocolates since 1928. One speciality: candied citrus peel in dark chocolate. It's part of the small nuts-and-sweets district centred on Karageorgi Servias.

❻ History Underground

Tucked amid chain coffee bars, the entrance to the basement of **Koraï 4** (http://korai4.gr) is easy to miss. During German occupation in WWII the Gestapo used these rooms as holding cells, and the walls are scratched and sketched with messages from prisoners.

❼ Time Machine Bar

Another shopping-arcade secret: **Galaxy Bar** (www.facebook.com/ GalaxyBarAthens), a lovely vintage place that, when it opened in the 1970s, was considered truly modern because it had a proper European-style stand-up bar. Its current style can be summarised in the framed photos of the Rat Pack and Franz Kafka.

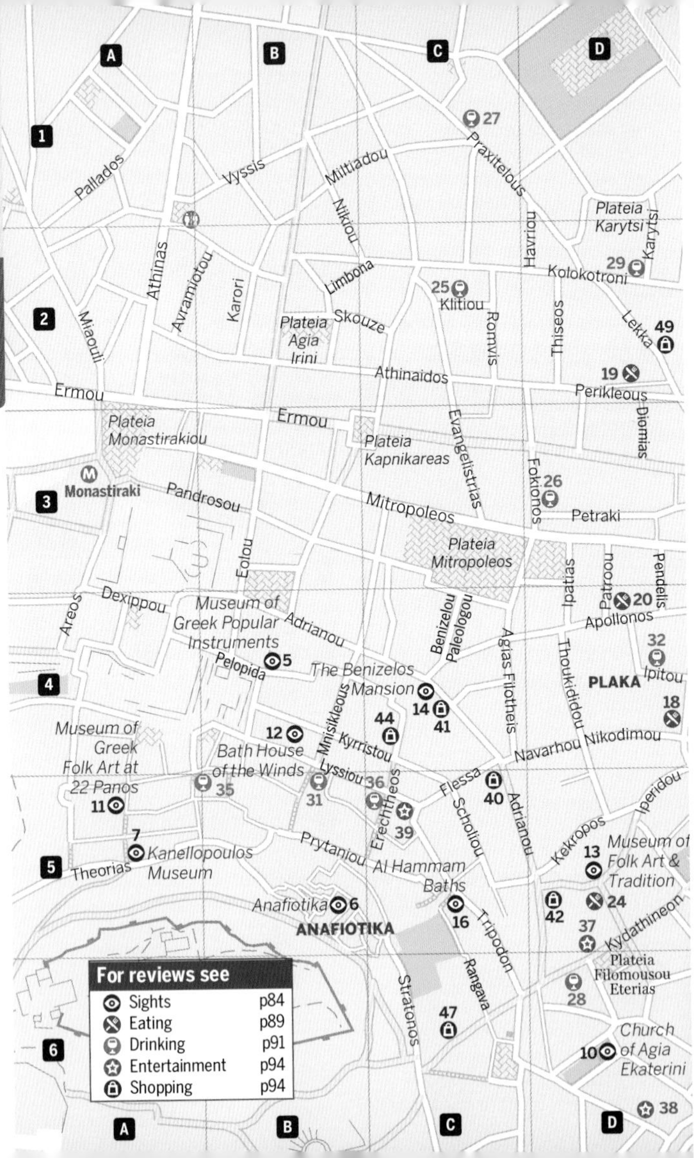

A **B** **C** **D**

1

Pallados

Vyssis

Miltiadou

Praxitelous

27

Plateia
Karytsi

Karytsi

2

Miaouli

Athinas

Avramiotou

Karori

Nikiou

Limbona

Skouze

Plateia
Agia
Irini

Klitiou

25

Romvis

Haritos

Kolokotroni

29

Thiseos

Lekka

49

19

Perikleous

Diomias

Ermou

Ermou

Athinaidos

Athinaidos

Plateia
Monastirakiou

Plateia
Kapnikareas

Evangelistrias

Fokionos

26

Petraki

3 Monastiraki

Pandrosou

Eolou

Mitropoleos

Plateia
Mitropoleos

Areos

Dexippou

Museum of
Greek Popular
Instruments

Adrianou

Benizelou
Paleologou

Agias Filotheis

Ipatias

Patroou

Apollonos

20

Pendelis

4

Pelopida

5

The Benizelos
Mansion

14

41

Thoukididou

Ipitou

32

PLAKA

18

Museum of
Greek
Folk Art at
22 Panos

11

12

Bath House
of the Winds

35

Mnisikleous

Kyrristou

Lyssiou

44

31

36

Erechtheos

Flessa

Scholiou

40

Adrianou

Navarhou Nikodimou

Iperidou

7

Kanellopoulos
Museum

Prytaniou

39

Al Hammam
Baths

Kekropos

13

Museum of
Folk Art &
Tradition

24

42

37

Kydathineon

Plateia
Filomousou
Eterias

5 Theorias

Anafiotika 6

ANAFIOTIKA

16

Tripodon

Rangava

28

Church
of Agia
Ekaterini

Stratonos

47

10

38

6

For reviews see

⊙ Sights   p84
✕ Eating   p89
🍷 Drinking   p91
★ Entertainment   p94
🔒 Shopping   p94

A **B** **C** **D**

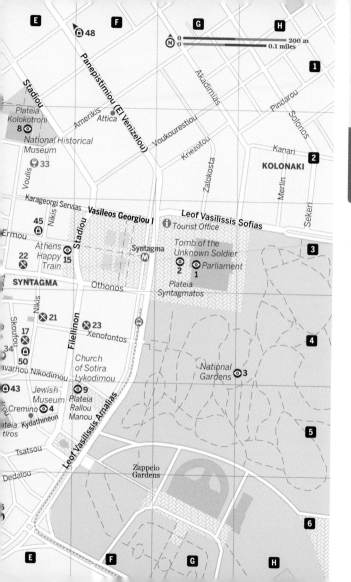

E F G H

🔒 48

Panepistimiou (El Venizelou)

Stadiou

Plateia
Kolokotroni
8 ◎

National Historical
Museum
❓ 33

Amerikis Attica

Akadimias

Pindarou

Solonos

Voukourestiou

Kriezotou

Zalokosta

Kanari

Merlin

Sekeri

KOLONAKI

Voulis

Karageorgi Servias

Vasileos Georgiou I

Nikis

Stadiou

Leof Vasilissis Sofias

ℹ Tourist Office

45
🔒

Ermou

Athens ◎
22 Happy
❌ Train
15

Syntagma
Ⓜ

Tomb of the
Unknown Soldier
◎ ◎ Parliament
2 1

SYNTAGMA

Othonos

Plateia
Syntagmatos

Nikis

❌ 21

Filellinon

❌ 23
Xenofontos

Skoufou

17
❌

34
🔒

50

avarhou Nikodimou

Church
of Sotira
Lykodimou

🔒 43

Jewish
Museum
◎ 4

Plateia
Rallou
Manou

◎ 9

National
Gardens ◎ 3

Cremino

ateia Kydathineon
tiros

Leof Vasilissis Amalias

Tsatsou

Dedalou

Zappeio
Gardens

N 0   200 m
   0   0.1 miles

1

2

3

4

5

6

Local Tips: Best Places for a Run in Athens

○ **Apostolou Pavlou promenade to Filopappou Hill** Huge cobble-stoned sidewalk, perfect for a run from the Ancient Agora to the pathways on Filopappou Hill and the Dionysiou Areopagitou walkway.

○ **National Gardens** (p85) Lush landscape with more than 7000 trees, 519 different kinds of plants and six ponds. Insider tip: the garden closes at sunset. If you're running around this time, stay earphone-free so you can hear the whistle signalling the gates are about to close.

○ **Panathenaic Stadium** (p122) Run the 500m racetrack on the rim of the marble stadium, the home of the first modern-day Olympic Games. Accessible only from the rear, through a green gate on Arhimidous, it is very much open and free to use, as long as you don't enter the actual stadium. Extra tip: from Arhimidous gate you can run up the green Ardettos Hill.

○ **Athens Riviera** Run, walk or swim at the Palaio Faliro seafront. The promenade of the Athens Riviera passes through Flisvos Marina, Palaio Faliro and Alimos to Glyfada. You can also swing through the Stavros Niarchos Park (p171) in Faliro.

○ **Olympic Stadium** Run around the Olympic Sports Complex in Marousi, used in the 2004 Olympics, and visit the Athens Olympic Museum.

Recommended by Margarita Kontzia,
Greek swimming champion and owner of fitness hotel Alkima,
www.alkimathens.com

Sights

Parliament
HISTORIC BUILDING

1 ⊙ MAP P82, G3

Built between 1836 and 1842 by Bavarian architect Friedrich von Gärtner, Greece's Parliament was originally the royal palace. From its balcony, the *syntagma* (constitution) was declared on 3 September 1843, and in 1935 the palace became the seat of parliament. The sessions can be visited and group tours booked; check online well ahead for the specific procedures. (www.hellenicparliament.gr)

Tomb of the Unknown Soldier
MONUMENT

2 ⊙ MAP P82, G3

In front of Parliament, the traditionally costumed *evzones* (presidential guards) stand by the tomb and change every hour on the hour. On Sunday at 11am, a whole platoon marches down Vasilissis

Sofias to the tomb, accompanied by a band. The *evzones* uniform of the *fustanella* (white skirt) and pom-pom shoes is based on the attire worn by the *klephts,* the mountain fighters of the War of Independence.

National Gardens

GARDENS

3 ⊙ MAP P82, H4

The former royal gardens, designed by Queen Amalia in 1838, are a pleasantly unkempt park that makes a welcome shady refuge from summer heat and traffic. Tucked among the trees are a cafe, a playground and turtle and duck ponds. The main entrance is on Leoforos Vasilissis Sofias, south of Parliament; you can also enter from Irodou Attikou to the east, or from the adjacent Zappeio Gardens (p123) to the south. (www.cityofathens.gr)

Jewish Museum

MUSEUM

4 ⊙ MAP P82, E5

This small museum traces the history of the Jewish community in Greece – starting with the deeply rooted Romaniote community established in the 3rd century BCE, through to the arrival of Sephardic Jews and beyond the Holocaust. The documents, religious art and folk objects are beautifully presented. Among the many fascinating pieces of history here is the story of Bishop Chrysostomos and Lucas Karrer, the mayor of

Zakynthos, who conspired to save the 275 Jews who lived on the island from Nazi round-ups. (www.jewishmuseum.gr)

Museum of Greek Popular Instruments

MUSEUM

5 ⊙ MAP P82, B4

A single avid ethnomusicologist collected almost 1200 folk instruments; the best are on display in three floors of this house-turned-museum. Headphones let visitors listen to the *gaïda* (Greek goatskin bagpipes) and the wood planks that priests on Mt Athos use to call prayer times, among other distinctly Greek sounds. Musical performances are held in the lovely garden in summer.

The Greek parliament

Anafiotika

AREA

6 ◎ MAP P82, B5

Clinging to the north slope of the Acropolis, the tiny Anafiotika district is a beautiful, architecturally distinct subdistrict of Plaka. In the mid-1800s, King Otto hired builders from Anafi to build a new palace.

In their homes here, they mimicked their island's architecture, all whitewashed cubes, bedecked with bougainvillea.

The area now is a clutch of about 40 homes, linked by footpaths just wide enough for people and roaming cats.

Enter on the west side near the Church of the Metamorphosis on Theorias. On the east side, zigzag up Stratonos.

Kanellopoulos Museum

MUSEUM

7 ◎ MAP P82, A5

A neoclassical mansion contains the collection of Paul and Alexandra Kanellopoulos that was bequeathed to the Greek state in the 1970s.

There's lovely classical and Byzantine art and jewellery, and especially transfixing terracotta and bronze classical figurines. Also note the ceilings in the Byzantine wing (the icons are great too).

Signage is a bit sparse but as the place is often empty of other visitors, it can feel like you're touring your own eclectic collection. (https://pacf.gr)

National Historical Museum

MUSEUM

8 ◎ MAP P82, E2

This grand old collection of swords, ship figureheads and portraits of moustachioed generals is a bit short on signage; it's best for people who already know something about modern Greek history and the many battles of the 19th century that built the nation, piece by piece.

This includes the battle of Messolongi, where Lord Byron fought; the museum owns the camp bed on which he died of malaria, among other effects.

There's also a wing of traditional jewellery and folk costumes. (www.nhmuseum.gr)

Church of Sotira Lykodimou

CHURCH

9 ◎ MAP P82, F5

First built in the 11th century and now the Russian Orthodox Cathedral, this is the only Byzantine church with an octagonal plan.

It's quite small but topped with a high dome, so the whole space, glittering with gold stars and icons, soars upward.

Neoclassical icons by the famed portrait painter Nikiforos Lytras (done when he was still a student at the School of Fine Arts in the mid-1800s) add a slightly uncanny realist touch.

Church of Agia Ekaterini

CHURCH

10 MAP P82, D6

One of the few very old Byzantine churches that is open regularly, this is definitely worth a peek inside to see how an 11th-century space is still in vibrant use and adorned with bright frescoes. For a time it was the property of the Monastery of St Catherine in the Sinai Peninsula, which is how it took on that saint's name. In the front yard are some Roman ruins.

Museum of Greek Folk Art at 22 Panos

MUSEUM

11 MAP P82, A5

While the new building for the main Museum of Greek Folk Art is being built, with a completion date

projected in 2024, this annexe houses the permanent collection *Men & Tools,* which is not quite as dry as it sounds. The small display, enhanced with music, is a loving tribute to Greeks' hard labour and refined skills in the preindustrial era. (www.mnep.gr)

Bath House of the Winds

MUSEUM

12 MAP P64, G6

One of the few remnants of Athens' Ottoman period, this 17th-century *hammam* (Turkish bath) is also the only intact historical public bath building in the city – however it unfortunately no longer functions as such. As a museum, though, it's quite attractive and atmospheric, with music, sound

Anafiotika

Syntagma & Plaka Sights

The Other Evzones

Guards in traditional dress are also posted along Irodou Attikou, behind the Parliament building, and it's fascinating to see them here, alone and away from tourist cameras, going through their ritual pomp – even in the dead of night.

and a few projections conjuring its glory days as you stroll through the various rooms. (www.mnep.gr)

Museum of Folk Art & Tradition   MUSEUM

13 🔘 MAP P82, D5

The 1920s mansion of folk-lorist Angeliki Hatzimichalis (1895–1965), who wrote more than 100 books and articles about Greek traditions, is a window into the daily life of yore. It's a pretty house and a nice dip into regional costumes, embroidery and more, along with family portraits. (www.opanda.gr)

The Benizelos Mansion   HOUSE

14 🔘 MAP P82, C4

The 17th-century Benizelos home is the oldest in Athens. A typical domestic structure from that period, it has dirt-floor downstairs rooms with wine and olive presses and wood-panelled living rooms upstairs. Look for the repurposed classical columns in the gate lead-ing to the backyard, formerly an olive grove. It's a nice free diversion, but note the limited opening hours. (www.archontiko-mpenizelon.gr)

Museum of Greek Children's Art   MUSEUM

Founded to cultivate a love of art and creative development, this space (see **43** 🔒 Map p82, E5) exhibits young artists' work and holds workshops for children. (www.childrensartmuseum.gr)

Athens Happy Train   TOURS

15 🔘 MAP P82, E3

This little red train-on-wheels is a bit goofy, but it's more city-friendly than a massive double-decker tour bus.

Stops include the Acropolis, Temple of Olympian Zeus and Panathenaic Stadium.

Tours take 40 minutes nonstop, or you can get on and off over the day. Trains leave from the top of Ermou every 30-40 minutes. (www.athenshappytrain.com)

Al Hammam Baths   BATHHOUSE

16 🔘 MAP P82, C5

Like the other two Turkish-style baths in Athens, this one is diminutive, but it is beautifully decorated in marble and tile and coloured chandeliers, to conjure an old-Ottoman atmosphere.

Moreover, it's set in a nice old house in Plaka, so after your steam and skin scrub, you can have tea on the terrace and admire the Acropolis. (https://alhammam.gr)

Eating

Avocado
VEGETARIAN €

17 🍴 MAP P82, E4

This popular cafe offers a full array of vegan, gluten-free and organic treats with an international spin. Next to an organic market, and with a tiny front patio, here you can enjoy everything from sandwiches to quinoa with aubergine, or mixed-veg coconut curry.

Juices and mango lassis are all made on the spot. (www.avocadoathens.com; 🛜 ✏️)

Evgenia
TAVERNA €€

18 🍴 MAP P82, D4

For great traditional fare, it's hard to beat this inconspicuous, no-frills taverna on the periphery of Plaka, with a few tables on the footpath. There's a standard menu but it's best to choose from the daily specials, which can include fresh seafood, such as prawn *saganaki* (fried cheese).

Granello
PIZZA

19 🍴 MAP P82, D2

Beloved traditional Italian-style pizza is the order of the day at this little outfit tucked away on a

Al Hammam Baths

Traditional Ice Cream

The lovely proprietress at **Cremino** (Map p82, E5; www.facebook.com/cremino. athens) makes gelato and sorbet that's both intensely flavoured and incredibly light, using cow and buffalo milk. Flavours change daily, but look for creamy-chewy *kaïmaki*, a classic recipe with Chios mastic resin and orchid root.

small alley behind the main drag of Perikleous. There are some simple metal tables surrounded by murals for eating in, or order your pizza for takeout. (www.granellopizza.gr)

Aspro Alogo

TAVERNA €€

20 MAP P82, D4

Humble in appearance, a simple doorway tucked among office buildings and hotels, this rustic taverna serves excellent examples of traditional Greek dishes. The friendly family who runs it sources the freshest ingredients.

Shiraki

JAPANESE

21 MAP P82, E4

Friendly, efficient owners and staff keep the delicious Japanese food flowing. Sushi is pricey but fresh, and there are plenty of traditional options from udon to ton katsu. (www.shiraki.gr)

Tzitzikas kai Mermigas

MEZEDHES €€

22 MAP P82, E3

Greek merchandise lines the walls of this cheery modern place that sits smack in the middle of central Athens.

It serves a tasty range of delicious and creative dishes, such as honey-drizzled, bacon-wrapped Naxos cheese, to a bustling crowd of locals and tourists. (www.tzitzi kasmermigas.gr)

Brigante

ITALIAN €€

23 MAP P82, F4

Don't let the urban, busy-street setting fool you. This is pure slow cooking: the owners of this trattoria make their pizzas and pasta from scratch and serve it up with a smile.

It does close early for Greece, at 9pm. (www.facebook.com/brigante. cucina)

Glykys

MEZEDHES €

24 MAP P82, D5

In a quiet corner of Plaka, this low-key place with a shady front yard is mostly frequented by students and locals.

It has a tasty selection of mezedhes, including traditional dishes such as *briam* (oven-baked vegetable casserole, only available in the evening) and cuttlefish in wine. (www.glykys.gr)

Drinking

Baba Au Rum
COCKTAIL BAR

25 MAP P82, C2

As the name implies, the focus here is on rum drinks, with an excellent selection of rarer Caribbean rums and a whole range of other creative cocktails, from classic tiki drinks to new inventions. This is just one of a handful of good little bars on this strip. (www.babaaurum.com)

Heteroclito
WINE BAR

26 MAP P82, D3

This relaxed wine bar, all mismatched vintage furniture and street seating, showcases the best of Greek vintages, paired with Greek cheeses and cold cuts. It periodically organises tasting events. The name is Greek for 'maverick'. (www.heteroclito.gr)

The Clumsies
BAR

27 MAP P82, C1

Look for the red neon in the hallway of this discreet bar that fills your coffee and creative cocktail needs.

Founded by award-winning bartenders, it's very serious about its drinks, but the atmosphere is definitely fun, and full of slick, handsome types on the weekends. You can also reserve The Room, a cosy enclave upstairs for six to 10 people. (www.theclumsies.gr)

Brettos
BAR

28 MAP P82, D6

Plaka is short on bars in general, but Brettos, both a bar and a distillery, makes up for it. More than a century old, its walls glow with stacks of multicoloured bottles and huge barrels.

Sample its home brands of wine, ouzo, brandy and other spirits. (https://brettosplaka.com)

Barley Cargo
BAR

29 MAP P82, D2

If you think Greek beer begins and ends with Alfa, head here to learn more. The big open-front bar stocks the products of many Greek microbreweries, as well as more than 100 international beers. Live music is a bonus. (www.facebook.com/BarleyCargo)

Stoa Life

Take any chance you get to duck into the *stoas* (shopping arcades) that cut through large buildings around Syntagma. Away from the street, where rent is cheaper, you might find old-man *ouzeries* (places serving ouzo and snacks), single-purpose stores, a jewel-box cocktail bar, even an occasional pop-up DJ party. Stairs down to basement level are often fruitful too.

ARON M/SHUTTERSTOCK ©

Brettos (p91)

Loser BAR

30 MAP P82, E4

Teeny, tiny with just a few stools out front, it fills up with chatting folks enjoying this quiet corner of busy downtown Athens. Music is chill, staff friendly and drinks on point.

Yiasemi CAFE

31 MAP P82, B5

Proof that Plaka is still very much a Greek neighbourhood despite the tourists, Yiasemi attracts a good mix of young Athenians, who set up for hours in the big armchairs or out on the scenic steps.

It's better by day (especially for the great veg breakfast buffet) and on weeknights, when it's not overwhelmed by the scene at other nearby restaurants. (www.yiasemi.gr)

Kiki de Grece WINE BAR

32 MAP P82, D4

Man Ray's muse, Kiki de Montparnasse, declared that in hard times all she needed was bread, an onion and a bottle of red wine.

This pedestrian-street bar also takes her as its muse, and offers plenty more than a bottle of red.

There's a huge range from Greece's vintners, paired with seasonal dishes from around Greece. (www.facebook.com/kikidegrece)

Seven Jokers

BAR

33 🚇 MAP P82, E2

Lively and central Seven Jokers has lovely old wood and brass fittings, plus a hip selection of wine and cocktails. (www.instagram.com/the7jokersbar.athens)

Oinoscent

WINE BAR

34 🚇 MAP P82, E4

Ignore the corny punning name – the team at this combo wine shop and bar are wise in the ways of the grape in all its varieties, whether Greek or international. (www.oinoscent.gr)

Klepsidra

CAFE

35 🚇 MAP P82, B5

Tucked away in a delightfully quiet spot on the west end of Plaka, with shady outdoor tables and friendly service,

Klepsidra is a favourite with locals before and after work; it's also an ideal rest spot after serious sightseeing.

It has a small selection of snacks (€4), such as *spanakopita* (spinach pie), though it's really about the atmosphere. (www.facebook.com/klepsidracafe)

Melina

CAFE

36 🚇 MAP P82, C5

A tribute to the great Mercouri, this cafe-bar is decorated with images of the actress and politi-

Syntagma & Plaka Drinking

The old district of Plaka

KITE_RIN/SHUTTERSTOCK ©

cian who lobbied for the repatriation of the missing Parthenon marbles.

Mercouri's most famous for the film *Never on Sunday,* but in fact that's a great day to come here, when it's very busy and prime outdoor seats offer a view of the Plaka parade.

Entertainment

Cine Paris   CINEMA

37 ⭐ MAP P82, D5

The Paris was established in the 1920s and it's still a magical place to see a movie. On a rooftop in Plaka, it offers great views of the Acropolis from some seats. (www.cineparis.gr)

Perivoli tou Ouranou   TRADITIONAL MUSIC

38 ⭐ MAP P82, D6

A favourite Plaka music haunt with dinner (fixed menus €40 to €50). (www.facebook.com/toperivolitou ouranou)

Greek Fashion

The upmarket department store **Attica** (Map p82, F2; www.atticadps.gr) stocks some of the best local designers (crafted-in-Greece Zeus + Dione, for instance), and its sale racks are good for restocking your travel wardrobe.

Stamatopoulos   TRADITIONAL MUSIC

39 ⭐ MAP P82, C5

This Plaka restaurant, established in 1882, has live music from 7pm to 1am. It is now so legendary that it can feel a bit like a film set. The crowd – spread over two garden-like levels outside or in the cosy, mural-covered dining room inside – gets more local as the night wears on. (www.stamatopoulo stavern.gr)

Shopping

Flâneur   DESIGN

40 🔒 MAP P82, C5

This cute shop has a tightly curated collection of souvenirs and travel gear. Get your hand-stamped 'φλανέρ' (that's 'flâneur' spelled in Greek) notebooks and your feta-tin patches and pins here. Even stocks vinyl by Greek indie bands. (www.facebook.com/ flaneursouvenirsandsupplies)

Forget Me Not   GIFTS & SOUVENIRS

41 🔒 MAP P82, C4

This impeccable small store (two shops, one upstairs and one down around the corner) stocks super-cool gear, from fashion to housewares and gifts, all by contemporary Greek designers.

Great for gift shopping – who doesn't want a set of cheerful 'evil eye' coasters or some Hermes-winged beach sandals? (www.forgetmenotathens.gr)

Athens: Economic Crisis & Recovery

In Athens' busy streets and lively cafes you may not immediately see *i krisi* – the financial crisis that Greeks have been labouring under since 2010. Conditions here are improving, but tax hikes and drastic pension cuts – imposed as terms of a series of bailout loans from the EU and the International Monetary Fund – have touched almost everyone and widened Greece's economic divide.

Homelessness, suicide, drug use and once-rare burglary and violent crime have risen. Young Greeks, usually highly educated, faced a youth unemployment rate of about 45%, though that has started to improve, with the number about 37% in 2021.

The most chaotic point may have been the near-collapse of banks in 2015, and the baffling about-face of anti-austerity prime minister Alexis Tsipras, who signed another bailout deal just three days after the public voted a resounding 'no' in a referendum. Mass strikes and violent clashes with the police followed. Around the same time, refugees fleeing conflict and persecution in Syria, Iraq, Afghanistan, Eritrea and various countries in West Africa began arriving in Greece by the thousands every day. For a time, the port of Piraeus and Plateia Viktoria were informal encampments. Immigrants make up about 11% of the region's population, and indeed, immigration, which first started in earnest in the 1990s, has reinvigorated some neighbourhoods.

As for the economic forecast, as of March 2022 overall unemployment was 12.8% – a 12-year low. And after the worst of the Covid-19 pandemic lockdowns in 2020 and 2021, tourism is rebounding with enormous vigour. Pre-pandemic tourist income was at an all-time high in 2019 at over €18 billion, climbed back to more than €10 billion in 2021 and in 2022 looked to be record-setting (at the time of writing). Nevertheless, while the economy is recovering, inflation and uncertainty mean nothing is guaranteed.

Ioanna Kourbela

FASHION & ACCESSORIES

 42 🔒 MAP P82, D5

Classic, cool fashion by a Greek designer with a preference for natural fibres.

Think elegantly draped cottons and silks in natural, warm tones and slouchy casual wear for the street.

She also has a couture collection available to view by appointment. (https://ioannakourbela.com)

NEJDET DUZEN/SHUTTERSTOCK ©

Adrianou Street

Amorgos ARTS & CRAFTS

43 MAP P82, E5

Charming store crammed with wooden toys, *karagiozi* (shadow puppets), ceramics, embroidery and other Greek folk art, as well as carved wooden furniture all made by the owner. (www.amorgosart.gr)

Alexis Papachatzis JEWELLERY

44 MAP P82, C4

This charming jewellery store is a delight before you even enter: turn the handle on the window display and watch as gears and pulleys animate the scene.

Papachatzis' designs have a storybook quality: small figures, clouds and animals rendered in sterling silver, bronze and enamel. (www.alexisp.gr)

Korres COSMETICS

45 MAP P82, E3

Many pharmacies stock some of this popular line of natural beauty products, but you can get the full range at the company's original location, where it grew out of a homeopathic pharmacy. (www.korres.com)

Eleni Marneri Galerie JEWELLERY

46 MAP P82, E6

Sample rotating exhibitions of local modern art and some of the best jewellery in the city. Handmade, unusual and totally eye-catching. (www.elenimarneri.com)

Finewine

WINE

47 🔒 MAP P82, C6

In the winding streets of Plaka, the finest wines can be found on this small lane with a small clutch of tables for sampling the wares. It's a welcoming destination for the curious and for local wine lovers who come to browse the rows of vintage Greek wines lining the centuries-old stone walls. (www.finewine.gr)

Xylouris

MUSIC

48 🔒 MAP P82, F1

Set in an arcade with several other music shops, this treasure trove is run by the family of legendary Cretan composer Nikos Xylouris.

They can guide you through the comprehensive range of Greek music CDs and DVDs, as well help with purchasing a new bouzouki if that's what you want.

Also has a branch at the Museum of Greek Popular Instruments (p85). (http://xilouris.gr)

Actipis

JEWELLERY

49 🔒 MAP P82, D2

Spiros Actipis designs elegant jewellery using materials such as smooth pebbles, gleaming silver and raw leather.

The shop closes during the summer, as Spiros decamps to

Best Shopping Streets

○ **Adrianou** Lined with souvenir shops – many generic, but still quite a number stocking interesting new designs. Shops here are generally open late.

○ **Ermou** Athens' first modern street of shops, and now mostly chains, but nice to stroll because it's car-free. It's named for Hermes, god of trade; nearly every Greek town has its own Ermou St.

Mykonos. (www.facebook.com/actipisjewellery)

Aidinis Errikos

ARTS & CRAFTS

50 🔒 MAP P82, E4

Artisan Errikos Aidinis' unique metal creations are made in his workshop at the back of this charming store, including small mirrors, candlesticks, lamps, aeroplanes and his signature bronze boats. (www.facebook.com/Errikos.Aidinis)

Anavasi

MAPS

51 🔒 MAP P82, E4

Great travel bookshop with an extensive range of Greece maps and walking and activity guides. (www.anavasi.gr)

Walking Tour 🥾

Central Athens Meander

Boisterous, monument-packed central Athens is best explored on foot. The historic centre, as well as the main archaeological sites, major landmarks, museums and attractions, are close to one another. The main civic hub of Athens, Plateia Syntagmatos, merges into the historic Plaka and Monastiraki neighbourhoods, which mesh one into the next, and make for a super stroll in which to soak up a bit of city-centre life.

Walk Facts

Start Plateia Syntagmatos

End Monastiraki Flea Market

Length 2.5km; three hours

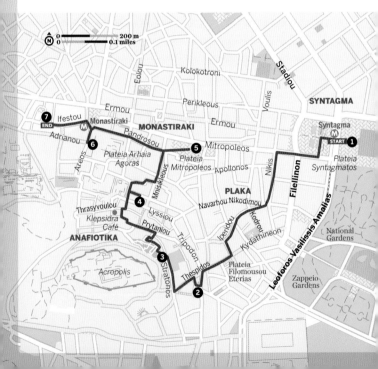

❶ Plateia Syntagmatos

This square, named for the *syntagma* (constitution) granted on 3 September 1843, is considered the centre of Athens. Time your visit with the changing of the guard at the **Tomb of the Unknown Soldier** (p84). North of the metro entrance, look for a section of the ancient cemetery and the Peisistratos aqueduct.

❷ Lysikrates Monument

Built in 334 BCE, this carved marble pedestal was the base for a bronze tripod trophy, awarded to winners of a dramatic contest. In ancient times, this street, Tripodon, was lined with such monuments, all the way to the Theatre of Dionysos at the foot of the Acropolis.

❸ Anafiotika Quarter

On Stratonos, which skirts the Acropolis, rises the **Church of St George of the Rock**, which marks the entry to Anafiotika (p86), an especially picturesque corner of Plaka.

❹ Turkish Baths

Duck into the **Bath House of the Winds** (p87), a pretty, late-Ottoman-era *hammam* restored as a museum. Around the corner, the gift shop of the **Museum of Greek Popular Instruments** (p85) is built atop the ruins of another set of baths.

❺ Plateia Mitropoleos

Jaunt north to Plateia Mitropoleos, where you'll find **Athens Cathedral** (p67) and its smaller, more historically significant neighbour, 12th-century **Church of Agios Eleftherios** (p67; known as the Little Metropolis), which was built from bits and pieces of ancient temples and earlier Christian monuments.

❻ Hadrian's Library

Pandrosou, a relic of the old Turkish bazaar, is full of souvenir shops and leads to Hadrian's Library (p67), once the most lavish public building in the city, erected by the eponymous Roman emperor around 132 CE.

❼ Monastiraki Flea Market

Cut through the main square at Monastiraki, which teems with street vendors, and head down Ifestou to the antiques dealers clustered around Plateia Avyssinias. The whole area is known as the Monastiraki Flea Market (p63) and the portion around Plateia Avyssinias is especially packed with interesting wares.

✕ Take a Break

Midway along the route, on the western edge of Plaka, **Klepsidra** (p93) is a delightfully quiet cafe that's popular with locals before and after work.

Explore
Kolonaki

Kolonaki is an adjective as much as a district: chic, stylish, elite. The area, which stretches from near Syntagma to the slopes of Lykavittos Hill, is where old money mixes with the nouveau fashionistas. For visitors, it's also home to excellent museums and an orderly, verdant district of top boutiques. Come here to sample Athens' good life...and maybe buy some shoes.

The Short List

o **Benaki Museum of Greek Culture (p102)** *Treating yourself to all the beauty of Greece, from ancient times through to the early 20th century.*

o **Byzantine & Christian Museum (p108)** *Descending into these, well, byzantine halls, each filled with more dazzling gold than the last.*

o **Museum of Cycladic Art (p108)** *Seeing the magnificently spare marble figures carved more than 4000 years ago.*

o **Lykavittos Hill (p105)** *Zipping up the so-called 'Hill of the Wolves' in a funicular and admiring the city view.*

o **(Window) shopping (p114)** *Wandering Kolonaki's shady streets and admiring the latest from Greek designers, such as Katerina Ioannidis.*

Getting There & Around

Ⓜ Evangelismos (blue line) for the eastern extents of Kolonaki.

Ⓜ Syntagma (blue and red lines) for the western edge.

Kolonaki Map on p106

Mount Lycabettus APOSTOLIS GIONTZIS/SHUTTERSTOCK ©

Top Experience 📷

Immerse Yourself at the Benaki Museum of Greek Culture

Antonis Benakis was a politician's son born in Alexandria, Egypt, in the late 19th century. After decades of collecting, in 1930 he turned the family's house into a museum. Now three storeys and many rooms larger, the museum presents all facets of Greek culture through the ages, with just the right amount of everything, and all of it beautiful.

◎ MAP P64

www.benaki.org

Ground Floor

Flint Flakes

In room 1, these shards of flint chipped into tool shapes date from 50,000–40,000 BCE, in the Middle Paleolithic period – maybe the oldest human-made thing you'll ever see.

Cretan School Painters

In gallery 12, the last room on the ground floor, are masterpieces from Venetian-held Crete (15th–16th centuries). These include works by Domenikos Theotokopoulos (later known as El Greco, 1541–1614), and several by Theodoros Poulakis (1622–92). The Cretan School developed techniques still used in icons today: sharp outlines, a geometric depiction of fabrics and subtly highlighted skin tones.

First Floor

Kozani Rooms

The rooms dedicated to the wealth of 18th- and 19th-century Epiros, themselves quite dazzling, lead into two reception halls that have been relocated from mansions in neighbouring Kozani, Macedonia. They are confections of carved and painted wood and stained glass.

Folk Costumes

Also on the 1st floor is room upon room of the finest and most intricately fashioned Greek traditional clothing, showing the diversity of the islands and the various regions of the mainland, including the Peloponnese, Epiros, Macedonia and Thrace. The spacious displays are interspersed with other priceless objects, such as carved marble door frames and jewel-encrusted Ottoman crowns.

★ Top Tips

o Thursday is a prime day to visit: the museum is open till midnight and free from 6pm on.

o A €30 pass is valid for one visit to each of the Benaki museums – including the modern/contemporary 138 Pireos St (p163) and the Museum of Islamic Art (p163), plus seven other smaller sites – over three months.

✕ Take a Break

The Benaki's cafe (p111) is renowned for great food in an open dining room, stretching out onto a terrace overlooking the National Gardens and the Acropolis.

Otherwise, pop over to one of Plateia Kolonakiou's cafes, such as Da Capo (p113).

Walking Tour 🥾

People-Watching in Kolonaki

If you're familiar with any Greek celebrities, you'll have a chance of spotting them in Kolonaki, a wealthy neighbourhood favoured by actors, politicians and journalists who prefer city life to the suburbs. Even if you don't recognise anyone, you can still admire a parade of aristocrats and fashionistas, all focused on key Kolonaki goals: looking and feeling good.

Walk Facts

Start Skoufa at Lykavittou

End Dinokratous near Plateia Dexameni

Length 1.8km; two hours

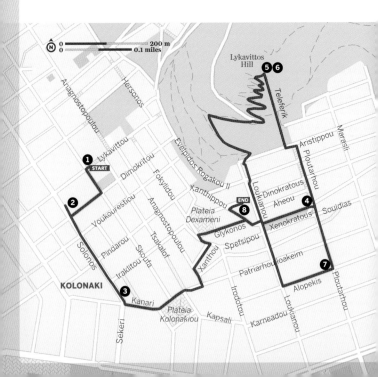

❶ Coffee Klatch

The extended people-watching session – with coffee on the side – is a Kolonaki pastime. Its historical roots are at **Filion** (www.filioncafe.com; 📶), where, to hear some tell it, decades of political schemes have been hatched (especially back when it was called Dolce). Now it's where the neighbourhood's old guard reads the day's paper.

❷ House Beautiful

A beautifully restored 19th-century mansion designed by Ernst Ziller now houses the **Allouche Benias Gallery** (http://allouchebenias.com). There's usually a couple of different shows a year with contemporary pieces in all media by both international artists and local talents alike.

❸ Spa Day

Learn more secrets of the jet set at **Apivita** (www.apivita.com), the boutique for the Greek brand's bee-products-based cosmetics and other products. A facial at the upstairs spa is a treat.

❹ Traditional Taverna

Filippou (www.filippou.gr) is always packed with locals enjoying the renowned homestyle fare that this classic taverna has been dishing out since 1923.

White-linen-covered tables spill into the courtyard, but book ahead to ensure you get one.

❺ Lykavittos Hill

From the top of Loukianou, a path leads up Kolonaki's **hill** (www.lycabettushill.com) for panoramas of the city and the Attic basin. Alternatively, take the **funicular** (www.lycabettushill.com) from the top of Ploutarhou.

❻ Peak Experience

Perched on the summit of Lykavittos is the little **Chapel of Agios Georgios**, which at night is floodlit like a beacon over the city. If you're lucky, you'll get there when a wedding is happening.

❼ Streetside Dinner

At a pavement table at modern taverna **Oikeio** (p110) you get the best of both worlds: excellent, affordable homestyle cooking and a view on street life, especially as the jet set is heading out and about. Book ahead on weekends for dinner, as it always fills up.

❽ Intimate Nightcap

Retreat to Kolonaki's upper reaches at the cosy **Jazz in Jazz** (p112), perfect for a last glass of wine or whisky. Everyone looks gorgeous in the glow of candles glinting off the brass instruments that decorate the walls.

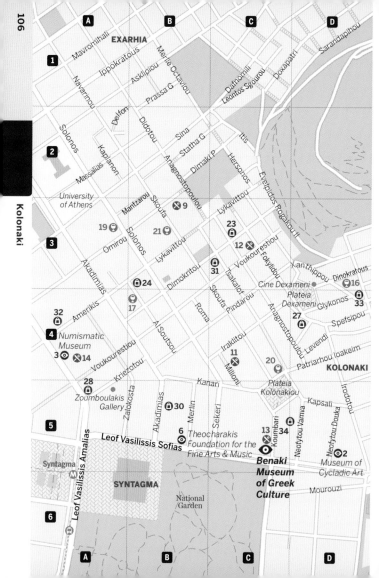

Kolonaki

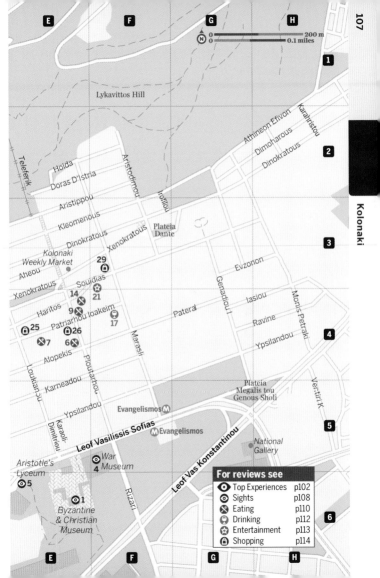

Lykavittos Hill

200 m
0.1 miles

Teleferik
Holda
Doras D'Istria
Aristodimou
Irofliou
Aristippou
Kleomenous
Dinokratous
Xenokratous
Plateia Dante
Athineon Efivon
Karahristou
Dimoharous
Dinokratous

Kolonaki Weekly Market
Aheou
Xenokratous
Souidias
14
9
21
Haritos
25
Patriarhou Ioakeim
26
7
6
Alopekis
Evzonon
Pateral
Genadiou I
Iasiou
Monis Petraki
Ravine
Ypsilandou
29
17
Marasli
Ploutarhou
Loukian.Ju
Karneadou
Ypsilandou
Karaoli-Dimitriou
Plateia Megalis tou Genous Sholi
Verdiri K.

Evangelismos M
Leof Vasilissis Sofias
M Evangelismos

Aristotle's Lyceum
5
War Museum
4
Rizari
Leof Vas Konstantinou
National Gallery

1
Byzantine & Christian Museum

For reviews see
◉	Top Experiences	p102
◎	Sights	p108
✖	Eating	p110
🍷	Drinking	p112
✪	Entertainment	p113
🛍	Shopping	p114

Sights

Byzantine & Christian Museum

MUSEUM

1 ◉ MAP P106, E6

This outstanding museum, based in the 1848 Villa Ilissia, offers exhibition halls, most of them underground in an expansive maze of glimmering gold and mosaics, crammed with religious art. The exhibits go chronologically, charting the gradual and fascinating shift from ancient traditions to Christian ones, and the flourishing of a distinctive Byzantine style. Of course there are icons, but also delicate frescoes (some salvaged from a church and installed on floating panels) and more personal remnants of daily life.

The villa grounds (free entry), which sit next to Aristotle's Lyceum, are a series of formal gardens that include ancient ruins, such as a section of the 6th-century-BCE Peisistratos aqueduct. A pretty cafe overlooks the greenery.

A joint ticket also covering the National Archaeological Museum (p130), Epigraphical Museum (p137) and Numismatic Museum costs €15 (€8 for students) and is valid for three days. (www.byzantine-museum.gr)

Museum of Cycladic Art

MUSEUM

2 ◉ MAP P106, A4

The 1st floor of this exceptional private museum is dedicated to the iconic minimalist marble Cycladic figurines, dating from 3000 BCE to 2000 BCE. They inspired many 20th-century artists, such as Picasso and Modigliani, with their simplicity and purity of form. Most are surprisingly small, considering their outsize influence, though one is almost human size. The rest of the museum features Greek and Cypriot art dating from 2000 BCE to the 4th century CE.

Overall, there's an interesting focus on how these objects were used, culminating in the 4th-floor exhibit, *Scenes from Daily Life in Antiquity,* where objects are set in photo recreations of ancient scenes. When you're full of history, check to see if there is an exhibition of contemporary art in the adjacent mansion – if so, it can be reached via the tunnel that's beside the museum's pleasant, modern **cafe** on the ground floor. There's also a **shop** selling stylish gifts. (https://cycladic.gr)

Numismatic Museum

MUSEUM

3 ◉ MAP P106, A4

The collection of coins here, dating from ancient through to modern times, is excellent, but of more general interest is the dazzling 1881 mansion in which it's housed. Built by architect Ernst Ziller, it was the home of Heinrich Schliemann, the archaeologist who excavated Mycenae and Troy; fittingly, its mosaic floors and painted walls and ceilings are covered in classical motifs. The adjoining gardens have an excellent **cafe**. (www.nummus.gr)

War Museum

MUSEUM

4  MAP P106, F5

This relic of the junta years is a stark architectural statement of the times. But its displays of weapons, maps, armour and models from the Mycenaean civilisation to the present day make an interesting break from the classics and there are some impressive pieces of kit parked around it, including fighter jets and an exact copy of the 1912 *Daedalus,* Greece's first military aircraft. (www.war museum.gr)

Aristotle's Lyceum

RUINS

5  MAP106, E6

Excavated only in 2011, this site is not much to look at – only building outlines are visible – but it is hallowed ground. Aristotle founded his school here, outside the city walls, in 335 BCE. He taught rhetoric and philosophy, and the place became known as a Peripatetic School, because teacher and pupils would walk as they talked. In the same way, you can make a circuit around the ruins breathing the air perfumed by fragrant plants. (http://odysseus.culture.gr)

The Byzantine And Christian Museum

MILAN GONDA/SHUTTERSTOCK ©

Byzantine Greece

The Byzantine Empire, which blended Hellenistic culture with Christianity, was established in 330 CE, when the Roman emperor Constantine I, a Christian convert, declared the city of Byzantium the empire's new capital – and changed its name to his own: Constantinople. As Rome went into terminal decline, this eastern capital, the centre of a Christian state, grew in wealth and strength.

As for Greece, it became officially Christian a bit later, in 394, and the worship of Greek and Roman gods was banned. Athens managed to remain an important cultural centre until 529, when the teaching of 'pagan' classical philosophy was finally forbidden, in favour of Christian theology.

The Byzantine Empire faced continued pressure from the Persians and Arabs, but held the core of its territory for many centuries. Athens, though, was no longer a centre, but an edge, and it faced attacks from the west. Between 1200 and 1450, the city was occupied by a succession of opportunistic Franks, Catalans, Florentines and Venetians. The empire finally fell in 1453, when the Turks captured Constantinople – and changed its name again, to İstanbul. Neglected, Athens didn't regain any kind of status until 1834, when it was declared the capital of the new Greek state.

Theocharakis Foundation for the Fine Arts & Music   ARTS CENTRE

6 ◎ MAP P106, B5

This arts centre has good exhibitions spread across three levels of gallery space; they change around four or five times a year. For English details on the exhibitions, download the app from Clio Muse (https://cliomusetours.com). Also here is a theatre that hosts occasional classical music performances and other events. (www.thf.gr)

Eating

Oikeio   MEDITERRANEAN €€

7 ✕ MAP P106, E4

With excellent homestyle cooking, this modern taverna lives up to its name (meaning 'homey'). It's decorated like a cosy bistro, and tables on the footpath allow people-watching without the usual Kolonaki bill. Pastas, salads and international fare are tasty, but try the daily *mayirefta* (ready-cooked meals), such as the excellent stuffed zucchini. Book ahead on weekends. (www.facebook.com/oikeio)

Kostarelos

CHEESE €

8 ⊗ MAP P106, E4

Fun fact: Greeks eat the most dairy in Europe, an average of 30kg per person per year. And when you visit Kostarelos, you might see why. The long-established family dairy business is now an elegant little deli and sandwich shop that caters to cheese lovers in all ways, whether it's *saganaki* (fried cheese), fondue or creative sandwiches. (www.kostarelos.gr)

Nice
n Easy

CAFE €€

9 ⊗ MAP P106, B3

Dig into fresh organic sandwiches, salads and brunch treats (such as *huevos rancheros*) beneath images of Louis Armstrong and Marilyn Monroe at this casual cafe. Lots of vegan and gluten-free options. (www.niceneasy.gr; ✎)

Kalamaki
Kolonaki

GREEK €

10 ⊗ MAP P106, E4

Order your pork or chicken by the *kalamaki* (skewer), add some salad and pittas, and you have great quick bites at this standout souvlaki joint.

It's small, but there's pavement seating for the requisite people-watching.

And, because it's Kolonaki, it's just a little more chic than average. (www.facebook.com/kalamaki.kolonaki)

M8

MEDITERRANEAN €€

11 ⊗ MAP P106, C4

On a quiet walking street tucked off the edge of Kolonaki's main square,

M8 has tables arranged out on the walkway and a lively atmosphere for its high-concept Mediterranean fare.

It's also a good candidate for cocktails and wine, with its solid list. (www.m8-athens.com)

Papadakis

SEAFOOD €€€

12 ⊗ MAP P106, C3

This understatedly chic restaurant, run by a well-known chef and cookbook author, specialises in traditional seafood, such as stewed octopus with honey and sweet wine, *salatouri* (fish salad) and sea salad (a type of green seaweed or sea asparagus). It's a bit formal, so not the place if all you want is a casual meal. (www.papadakisrestaurant.com)

Benaki Museum Cafe

GREEK €€

13 ⊗ MAP P106, C5

Traditional Greek food gets dressed up to match the museum (p102) setting, with an open dining room and terrace with a view of the National Gardens and the Acropolis.

It feels a bit clubby, with distinguished neighbours meeting for lunch, and it's open as late as the museum is, so you can have dinner or just a late drink here. Service can be spotty. (www.benaki.org)

Art Outings

Take the temperature of the local contemporary art scene at Kolonaki's many galleries. Stroll through **Allouche Benias** (p105) in the beautifully restored 1882 Deligeorgis Mansion, designed by Ernst Ziller. **Zoumboulakis Gallery** (Map p108, A5; www.zoumboulakis. gr) stocks a fine selection of limited-edition prints and posters by leading Greek artists, including Yannis Tsarouchis and Alekos Fassianos, and it also has a contemporary art space on Kolonaki's *plateia* (square).

Telemachos   STEAK €€€

14 🍴 MAP P106, A4

At this elegant modern chophouse, gorgeous dry-aged Piedmontese beef is on display – but great Greek dishes such as spit-roasted lamb are on the menu, too. Grilling is done over charcoal, service is smooth, and classic Greek film music sets a retro tone. Look for the pink neon sign at the end of the passage by Paul Patisserie. (www.telemachosathens.gr)

Capanna   ITALIAN €€

15 🍴 MAP P106, E4

Capanna hugs a corner, with tables wrapping around the footpath in summer. Cuisine is fresh Italian, from enormous pizzas to gnocchi

with gorgonzola. Enjoy hearty eating with attentive service and a goblet of wine. (www.capanna.gr; 🛜)

Drinking

Jazz in Jazz   BAR

16 🚇 MAP P106, D3

A good cool-weather destination, this cosy bar glows with candles and vintage brass instruments, and stays warm with the sounds of New Orleans jazz and neighbours chatting over a glass of wine or whisky. Closed August. (https:// jazzinjazz.business.site)

To Tsai   TEAHOUSE

17 🚇 MAP P106, B4

Get a Zen vibe as you sip from a vast range of teas from around the world at this minimalist tearoom and shop that's a calm respite in the midst of Kolonaki. (www.tea.gr; 🛜)

Buñuel Uptempo Bistro   CAFE

18 🚇 MAP P106, F4

Welcoming and cheerful, this low-key cafe-bar serves up great, rich Area 51 coffee by day and cocktails by night. (www.facebook.com/Bu nuelbar)

Dark Side of Chocolate   CAFE

19 🚇 MAP P106, A3

This tiny cafe has made a name for itself for its hot chocolate and handmade truffles, displayed like gems in a glass case. It's a tiny, cosy place for some restorative caffeine (there's coffee, too) and a sweet to nibble. (www.facebook.com/DarksideofChocolatebyAristotelis)

Da Capo

CAFE

20 MAP P106, C4

Da Capo anchors the cafes on Kolonaki's main square and is always mobbed. Unlike just about every other cafe in Greece, you have to order your coffee inside at the counter.

Passepartout

BAR

21 MAP P106, B3

This all-day cafe-bar is archetypal slick Kolonaki: modern decor, comfy seating and a see-and-be-seen attitude.

Outside tables fit the brunch set and by nightfall host a well-dressed crowd that spills onto the footpath.

It serves a good selection of Greek wines and microbrews as well as cocktails. (www.passepartout-cafe.gr)

Entertainment

Cine Athinaia

CINEMA

22 MAP P106, F3

This fair-season-only (May to early October) open-air cinema is set at the end of a short pedestrian street of pleasant bars.

There are usually two screenings per night at around 9pm and 11pm – check online for the schedule. (www.facebook.com/cine-athinaia.gr)

Jazz in Jazz

VANGELIS KORONAKIS/LONELY PLANET ©

Shopping

CAN
ART

23 MAP P106, C3

This innovative entry on the Kolonaki gallery scene, founded by art specialist Christina Androulidaki, has a stable of emerging and mid-career contemporary Greek and international artists. At the time of writing, it was relocating to a yet-to-be-determined space – check its website. (www.can-gallery.com)

Lemisios
SHOES

24 MAP P106, B3

An Athens classic, open since 1912, with timeless designs – T-straps, ballet flats, elegant Oxfords (its only style for men) – all custom-fit just for you. Bespoke designs are also possible. Considering the level of craft, this place is surprisingly affordable with sandals starting at €70. (www.lemisios.gr)

Prime Plateia

Plateia Dexameni has basically everything you need: a great little cafe, a view of an ancient ruin (part of the cistern from Hadrian's aqueduct, dramatically lit at night) and the classic open-air **Cine Dexameni** (Map p106, D3; www.cined exameni.gr), which has deck chairs and tables to rest your beer on.

Fanourakis
JEWELLERY

25 MAP P106, E4

One of the most creative and exciting Greek jewellers, Fanourakis designs delicate, quirky pieces: gold folded like pencil shavings, unicorn charms, pavé diamond rings like jagged rocks. The distinctive forms are sheer art. (www.fanourakis.gr)

Katerina Ioannidis
JEWELLERY

26 MAP P106, E4

From a family of goldsmiths, Ioannidis merges Greek and other global folkloric elements into jewellery that is light, elegant, bohemian and sometimes even a little funny: a pendant of, say, a gold-plated sheep's head set on a fuzzy black pompom, or a bean-shaped charm. (www.katerinaioannidis.com)

Elena Votsi
JEWELLERY

27 MAP P106, D4

Votsi is renowned for her big and bold designs using exquisite semiprecious stones. So sculptural is her work that she was selected to redesign the Olympic Games medals in 2004. She has branched out into handwoven bags and Greek-themed home items. (www.elenavotsishop.com)

Mastiha Shop
FOOD

28 MAP P106, A5

Mastic (*mastiha* in Greek), the medicinal resin from rare trees only found on the island of Chios, is the key ingredient in everything in this store, from natural skin products to a liqueur that's divine when served chilled. There's also an airport branch. (www.mastihashop.com)

Michalis Alexandrakis HEALTH & WELLNESS

29 🔒 MAP P106, F3

In the mould of the great Greek philosophers, Michalis Alexandrakis operates one of the best hair salons in Athens and shares wisdom along the way – perfect if you need a tune-up while on the road. He also offers a range of hair products, including Oway's organic hair care line. (www.facebook.com/alexandrakismichalis)

Vassilis Zoulias FASHION & ACCESSORIES

30 🔒 MAP P106, B5

An old-school designer, Zoulias crafts a couture line with colourful dresses inspired by the '50s and '60s and continues this theme in elegant, feminine shoes that are timeless. (www.vassiliszoulias.com)

Parthenis FASHION & ACCESSORIES

31 🔒 MAP P106, C3

Orsalia Parthenis continues the powerful design legacy of her father, Dimitris, creating high-quality, supersleek clothes in natural fibres. No frills, just sharp lines. For both men and women. (www.orsalia-parthenis.gr)

Street Market

See Kolonaki's practical side at its *laïki agora*, the weekly neighbourhood **fruit-and-vegetable market** (Map p106, E3; www.laikesagores.gr) that fills leafy Xenokratous with fresh produce, fish, olives, flowers and more.

Kombologadiko FASHION & ACCESSORIES

32 🔒 MAP P106, A4

If you're in the market for a very special set of that old-school Greek accessory, *komboloï* (worry beads), check this oh-so-elegant showroom. It stocks ready-made designs, some from industrial materials as well as semiprecious stones and amber, starting from as little as €7. (www.kombologadiko.gr)

Maison d'Olive FOOD

33 🔒 MAP P106, D4

Come worship at the temple of all things olive: from the fruit to the oil. There are tastings and accompaniments, too. (www.wmaisonolives.com)

Art Appel Gallery ART

34 🔒 MAP P106, D5

This below-street-level space has hosted shows of works by the likes of Vangelis Tzermias – known for his gestural seascapes – and there is an emphasis on bold abstraction. Exhibitions change every two months or so. (www.artappelgallery.gr)

Explore
Mets & Pangrati

East of the Acropolis, the Zappeio Gardens and the ruins of the Temple of Olympian Zeus lead to the elegant Panathenaic Stadium. On the hill above the stadium are the diverse, unpretentious districts of Mets, named for a brewery once headquartered here, and Pangrati, with some lovely neoclassical and prewar houses and low-key-cool places to eat.

The Short List

○ **National Gallery (p122)** *Cruising this brand new, state-of-the-art museum filled with Greece's national art collection.*

○ **Panathenaic Stadium (p122)** *Jogging around the track with the roar of the (imaginary) crowd in your ears, and posing for a photo on the Olympic medallists' stand.*

○ **Basil & Elise Goulandris Foundation (p122)** *Ogling exhibitions picked from this wonderful modern and contemporary European art collection in a superb gallery.*

○ **Athens' First Cemetery (p123)** *Admiring the work of some of Greece's finest neoclassical sculptors, which just happens to top the tombs of the city's rich and famous.*

Getting There & Around

Ⓜ Akropoli (red line) or Syntagma (blue and red lines) for the Temple of Olympian Zeus. Akropoli is closest to Mets.

Ⓜ Evangelismos (blue line) is also good for Pangrati.

🚌 Trolleybus 2, 4 or 11; these stop near the stadium and continue uphill to Plateia Plastira.

Mets & Pangrati Map on p120

Top Experience 📸
Marvel at the Temple of Olympian Zeus

You can't miss this mega-marvel, smack in the centre of Athens. Once the largest temple in Greece, it probably ranks among the most drawn-out projects in history, begun in the 6th century BCE and finished in 131 CE.

⊙ MAP P120, A3

Olympieio

📞 210 922 6330

http://odysseus.culture.gr

Leoforos Vasilissis Olgas

🕗 8am-3pm Oct-Apr, to 8pm May-Sep

Ⓜ Akropoli, Syntagma

Temple

Seven centuries after Peisistratos started it, Hadrian finished the temple by placing a giant gold-and-ivory statue of Zeus inside. Then he matched it with an equally large one of himself. Maybe his immodesty jinxed it: the very next century, the temple was destroyed when the Herulians (a Germanic tribe from near the Black Sea) sacked the city.

Columns

The temple was built with 104 Corinthian columns, each with a base diameter of 1.7m and standing 17m high. Only 15 remain, the rest having been repurposed over the centuries, so you'll have to put your imagination to work to envisage the temple's former scope. The one fallen column was blown down in a gale in 1852.

Original Temple

Hadrian's temple is built on the site of a smaller one (590–560 BCE), also dedicated to the cult of Olympian Zeus. Look closely: its foundations can still be seen.

Hadrian's Arch

Just outside the temple fence, at the corner of Leoforos Vasilissis Amalias, sits this lofty monument, erected as thanks to Roman emperor Hadrian, probably just after the temple was consecrated. The inscriptions laud the new Roman era: the northwest frieze reads, 'This is Athens, the Ancient city of Theseus', while the southeast frieze states, 'This is the city of Hadrian, and not of Theseus'.

Sanctuary of Pan

Outside the temple fence, to the south, explorers can find a slip of the Ilissos River (elsewhere covered by pavement) and, nearby, a rock-cut sanctuary to the god Pan, another Roman-era worship site.

★ Top Tips

o Admission to the site is included in the €30 Acropolis combo ticket.

o There is no shade: wear a hat and sunscreen and bring water.

o You can see most of the temple (and Hadrian's Arch) from outside the fence if you're rushed. Or peer down on it all from the rooftop bar at the **Athens Gate hotel** (www.athens-gate.gr; ❄ @ 🛜).

✗ Take a Break

For a healthy pick-me-up, head to Veganaki (p48), across the busy Athanasiou Diakou boulevard.

Walk up to Mets for a laid-back coffee at the Odeon Cafe (p126) and a spinach pie from the excellent bakery across the street.

Mets & Pangrati

N

0 — 200 m
0 — 0.1 miles

A

B

C

D

1

Leof Vasilissis Amalias

Roman
6 Baths

Zappeio
Palace

National
Gardens

Trodou Attikou

☆20

2

Zappeio
Gardens

⊙5

Leof Vasilissis Olgas

Leof Vasileos Konstantinou

Plateia
Stadiou

Temple of
Olympian
Zeus

Panathenaic 3
Stadium

3

Ardittou

Ardettos
Hill

Piga M

Theotoki

4

Miniati

Karea

Nerik

Anapafseos

Typteou

Glatkou

Gorgiou

Harvouri

Papatsoni

METS

Aristonikou

Sorvolou

Fotiadou

Balanou K

Longinou

17

Markou Mousourou

Trivonianou

Stratigou Rodiou

Arhimidous

Dikearhou

Alsos
Longinou

Stratigou Ioannou

Stratigou Domboli

5

Karea

Timoleondos

Voulgareos Evg

Malamou

19
☆

Efpompou

Trivonianou

Defner

4⊙ Athens' First
Cemetery

6

Leof Vouliagmenis

Iolis

Ilioupoleos

A

B

C

D

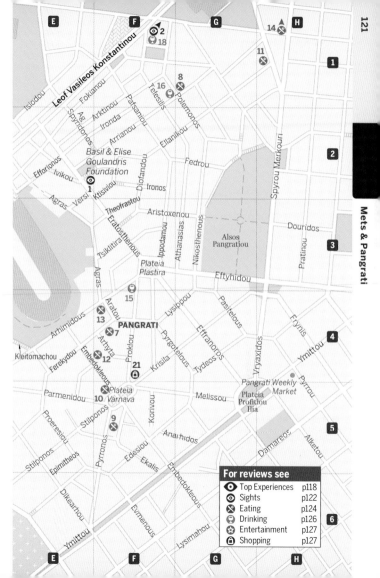

Mets & Pangrati

Olympic Morning Workout

Make like an Olympian and run laps or stairs in style inside the **Panathenaic Stadium** from 7.30am to 9am every morning. Sign a waiver (download from the website), pay admission and you're good to go.

Sights

Basil & Elise Goulandris Foundation MUSEUM

 1 MAP P106, E2

Opened in October 2019, this excellent museum of modern and contemporary art showcases the collection of shipping magnate Basil Goulandris and his wife Elise. Alongside pieces from the likes of top European artists, including Cézanne, Van Gogh, Picasso and Giacometti, are works from pioneering Greek painters such as Parthenis, Vasiliou, Hadjikyriakos-Ghikas, Tsarouchis and Moralis. (https://goulandris.gr)

National Gallery MUSEUM

2 MAP P106, F1

Greece's national art museum has reopened in a brand-new state-of-the-art complex. The spacious galleries are arranged chronologically and thematically, making a superb tour of Greek painting from the 19th century to the present, with some of the real master-pieces being in the 20th-century collection. See wonderful works by Ghikas, Parthenis, Tsarouchis and Tetsis, and ogle the views from the enormous plate-glass windows looking onto Lykavittos Hill. The sculpture collection is on view at the **National Sculpture Gallery** (www.nationalgallery.gr) in Goudi.

Panathenaic Stadium HISTORIC SITE

3 MAP P120, D3

With its serried rows of white Pentelic marble seats – enough for 70,000 spectators – built into Ardettos Hill, this ancient-turned-modern stadium is a draw both for lovers of classical architecture and sports fans imagining the roar of the crowds from millennia past. Built in the 4th century BCE and restored for the first modern Olympic games in 1896, it was first used as a venue for the Panathenaic athletic contests. It's said that at Hadrian's inauguration in 120 CE, a thousand wild animals were sacrificed in the arena. Later, the seats were rebuilt in marble by Herodes Atticus.

In 1895, after centuries of disuse, the stadium was restored by wealthy Greek benefactor Georgios Averof – you can see his portrait carved in marble to the right of the entrance. The running track and field is not modern Olympic-size, so the stadium was used only for archery and the marathon finish in the 2004 games. Now it's occasionally used for concerts and public events. A ticket gets you an audio tour, admission to a tiny exhibit on the modern Olympics (mainly eye-candy games posters) and the opportunity to take your photo on a winners' pedestal. (www.panathenaicstadium.gr)

Athens' First Cemetery

CEMETERY

4 ◉ MAP P120, B5

Under Ottoman rule, Greeks buried their dead at their local church. Only after independence in 1821 was this city cemetery established. It's a peaceful place to explore, with beautiful neoclassical sculptures, including *Sleeping Maiden* by Yannoulis Chalepas, the most admired Greek sculptor of the modern era. Famous people buried here include the Benaki family and the archaeologist Heinrich Schliemann (1822–90), whose mausoleum is decorated with scenes from the Trojan War.

Zappeio Gardens

GARDENS

5 ◉ MAP P120, B2

The southwestern third of the green space at the centre of Athens, adjacent to the National Gardens (p85), is a network of wide, tree-shaded walkways around the grand **Zappeio Palace** (www.zappeion.gr). The main entrances are on Leoforos Vasilissis Amalias and Leoforos Vasilissis Olgas.

The open-air Aegli Cinema (p127) is alongside the palace.

Mets & Pangrati Sights

Zappeion Hall

AERIAL-MOTION/SHUTTERSTOCK ©

Peisistratos the Dictator

The first seeds of Athenian democracy were sown when Solon became *arhon* (chief magistrate) in 594 BCE and improved the lot of the poor by forgiving debts and establishing a process of trial by jury.

This initial foray did not last, however. The reforms provoked unrest, and on the pretext of restoring stability, Peisistratos, head of the military, seized power in 560 BCE. He focused not on the people, but on Athenian might, building a formidable navy and extending the city's influence. He began work on the massive Temple of Olympian Zeus, built a massive aqueduct and inaugurated the Festival of the Great Dionysia, the precursor to Attic drama.

In 528 BCE, Peisistratos was succeeded by his son, Hippias, no less an oppressor. With the help of Sparta in 510 BCE, Athens rid itself of him, and entered into its golden age of philosophy, arts and, again, democracy.

Roman Baths

RUINS

6 MAP P120, A1

Excavation work to create a ventilation shaft for the metro uncovered the well-preserved ruins of a large Roman bath complex, built in the 3rd century CE where the Ilissos River once ran. A portion is exposed at the edge of the Zappeio Gardens.

Eating

Soil

GASTRONOMY €€€

7 ❌ MAP P120, F4

Magic happens behind the butter-yellow neoclassical facade of Soil, a new entry on Athens' culinary scene. Chef Tasos Mantis of Hytra fame has opened his own restaurant where he weds fresh-from-the-earth (as the name would suggest) vegetables, herbs and edible flowers with choice seafood and meats in a creative, contemporary tasting menu, with an available wine pairing. (www.soilrestaurant.gr)

Mavro Provato

MEZEDHES €€

8 ❌ MAP P120, G1

Book ahead for this wildly popular modern *mezedhopoleio* (mezedhes restaurant) in Pangrati, where tables line the sidewalk and delicious small (well, small for Greece) plates are paired with regional Greek wines. (Black Sheep; www.tomauroprovato.gr)

Spondi

MEDITERRANEAN €€€

9 MAP P120, F5

Athenians frequently vote two-Michelin-starred Spondi the city's best restaurant, and its Mediterranean haute cuisine, with a strong French influence, is indeed excellent. It's a lovely dining experience, in a relaxed setting in a charming old house with a bougainvillea-draped garden. Book ahead. (www.spondi.gr)

Kallimarmaro

BAKERY €

10 MAP P120, F5

Exceptionally good *spanakopita* (spinach pie) and other pies at this neighbourhood bakery – it's the breakfast go-to for many locals. Fills all your cream-puff needs too.

Athenais

GREEK €

11 MAP P120, H1

Little more than a kitchen with a few stools, this is a friendly spot for fresh, prepared Greek dishes like lentils, stuffed tomatoes, roast pork or beef with pasta. Browse the dishes behind the counter for a quick, cheap bite or takeaway. (www.facebook.com/12cda)

Colibri

PIZZA €

12 MAP P120, F4

Locals go here for the alleged best pizza in Athens. Pizzas range from classic Italian to creative vegetarian (seriously, the yoghurt works). Burgers and salads are also excel-lent. It's one of several fine eateries on a quiet tree-lined street.

Vyrinis

TAVERNA €

13 MAP P120, F4

This popular neighbourhood spot has been modernised a bit, but maintains its essential taverna-ness, with homestyle Greek food plus reliable house wine from big barrels at reasonable prices. On warm nights, all activity moves to the lovely courtyard garden, just up the side street. (www.facebook.com/VyrinisGreekTavern)

Vezené

GREEK €€€

14 MAP P120

One of Athens' best modern Greek bistros, Vezené is a relaxed affair where the waiters will bring to the table the catch of the day and glistening cuts of prime steak to explain the provenance and what goes into each dish. The wood-oven-baked pies are very good, as is the signature, deconstructed *pastitsio,* a kind of Greek lasagne. (http://vezene.gr;)

Pangrati's Market

Go deep in Pangrati to its *laïki agora* (weekly street market) on Fridays on Pirrou starting at Ymittou and heading southeast. Further on, Filolaou is a really typical, non-flashy Athens commercial strip.

Olympic History

The Olympic tradition emerged at the site of Olympia in the Peloponnese around the 11th century BCE as a paean to Zeus. Initially, it was footraces only, run by priests, priestesses and other notables. By the 8th century BCE, the festival had morphed into a major, male-only event that convened for five days every four years; the schedule alternated years with other regional competitions around Greece, a cycle referred to as the Panhellenic Games. This way, athletes could compete frequently. During the competition, city-states were bound by a sacred truce to stop any fighting underway.

Crowds of spectators lined the tracks, where competitors vied for victory in athletics, chariot races, wrestling and boxing. Unlike at Athens' Panathenaic contests, where winners received cash and valuable olive oil, the first prize at the Olympic Games was purely symbolic: a simple crown of olive leaves. (Laurel wreaths, now considered a symbol of victory, were awarded at the Pythian Games, one of the other regional competitions.) Ultimately, it was the esteem of the people that most mattered, for Greek Olympians were venerated. The ancient games ceased in 393 CE, when Emperor Theodosius I banned all pagan worship, and were revived in modern form in 1896.

Drinking

Chelsea Hotel   BAR

15   MAP P120, F3

When people talk about the cool-but-mellow scene in Pangrati, they're probably thinking of places like this cafe-bar on Plateia Plastira. By day it's about coffee and people reading or working on their laptops. When the sun sets, every seat is filled with young Athenians. (📶)

Millybird   CAFE

16   MAP P120, F1

This airy coffee shop with large glass windows dishes up top-notch baked goods and light snacks and serves robust coffee drinks on a quiet street in Pangrati. (www.facebook.com/MillybirdHouse)

Odeon Cafe   CAFE

17   MAP P120, C4

This corner cafe-bar is a delightful slice of local Athens life, where friends chat quietly beneath an ivy bower over the footpath. Extra-friendly staff, plus snacks and drinks. You may get lucky and find musicians jamming on the resident piano, double bass and guitar. (www.facebook.com/odeoncafe)

Epireia
CAFE

18   MAP P120, F1

One of several nice cafes on pretty, green Plateia Proskopon, this airy, colourful place has the unpretentious Pangrati vibe, plus solid food (pizza, burgers) and craft beers. It's a welcome endpoint if you've been exploring the neighbourhood. (www.facebook.com/epireia)

Entertainment

Half Note Jazz Club
JAZZ

19   MAP P120, B5

Athens' most serious jazz venue is a cosy place that hosts Greek and international musicians. Check the schedule, as it's not open every night and closes entirely in summer. (www.halfnote.gr)

Aegli Cinema
CINEMA

20   MAP P120, C2

This historical open-air cinema showed its first film in 1903. Set in the verdant Zappeio Gardens (p123), it's a bit quieter than others and has great fresh air. (www.facebook.com/aiglizappeion)

Shopping

Bakaliko
FOOD & DRINKS

21   MAP P120, F4

A one-stop shop for fine Greek food products, this traditional grocery store is decked with awards for its dedication and stock of olive oil, wine, cheese, nuts, yoghurt and honey. (http://paradosiakompakaliko.blogspot.com)

Traditional Greek store

DIMITRIS_K/AERIAL-MOTION/SHUTTERSTOCK

Explore

Omonia & Exarhia

Omonia is Athens' practical heart, a transit hub and location of administrative offices. It's not a destination, but you may pass through – perhaps on your way to neighbouring Exarhia and the National Archaeological Museum. Exarhia is famous for its squat scene and vocal anarchists, but also offers a fascinating mix of students (it's near the universities) and creative types, against a backdrop of intense graffiti and ever-present riot police.

The Short List

○ **National Archaeological Museum (p130)** *Marvelling at the skill of classical artists at this enormous treasure house. You'll almost certainly get footsore before you've seen everything.*

○ **Strefi Hill (p143)** *Enjoying the view over the city, as well as the chilled-out atmosphere at Exostrefis cafe.*

○ **Live music (p143)** *Stumbling on a small bar such as Feidiou 2 Music Cafe, with a couple of musicians and a crowd that sings along with every word.*

○ **Cretan food (p138)** *Sampling one of Greece's proudest and most diverse regional cuisines at I Kriti or another one of the excellent restaurants here.*

Getting There & Around

Ⓜ Omonia (red and green lines) sits due west of Exarhia.

Ⓜ Panepistimio (red line) for southern Exarhia.

🚌 Trolleybus 2, 4, 5, 9 or 11 from anywhere on Panepistimiou to Polytechnio stop, in front of the archaeological museum.

Omonia & Exarhia Map on p1362

Omonia square MARIANNA IANOVSKA/SHUTTERSTOCK ©

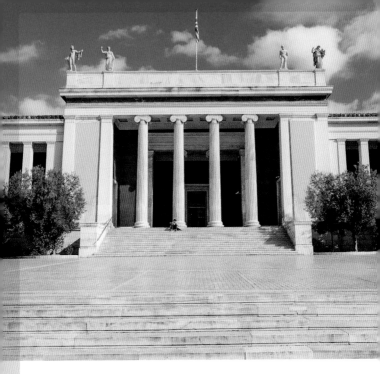

Top Experience 📷
Admire Antiquities at the National Archaeological Museum

The National Archaeological Museum houses the world's finest collection of Greek antiquities. The enormous 19th-century neoclassical building holds room upon room filled with more than 10,000 examples of sculpture, pottery, jewellery, frescoes and more. You simply can't appreciate it all in one go – but whatever you do lay eyes on will be a treat.

◉ MAP P136, D1

☎ 213 214 4800

www.namuseum.gr

adult/child €10/free
mid-Apr–Oct' €5/free
Nov–mid-Apr

🚌 2, 3, 4, 5 or 11 to Poly-techneio, Ⓜ Viktoria

Mycenaean Antiquities – Gallery 4

Directly ahead as you enter the museum is the **prehistoric collection**, showcasing some of the most important pieces of Mycenaean, Neolithic and Cycladic art, many in solid gold. The fabulous collection of Mycenaean antiquities is the museum's tour de force. This great death mask of beaten gold is commonly known as the **Mask of Agamemnon**, the king who, according to legend, attacked Troy in the 12th century BCE – but this is hardly certain. Heinrich Schliemann, the archaeologist who set to prove that Homer's epics were true tales, and not just myth, unearthed the mask at Mycenae in 1876.

Vaphio Cups

The exquisite Vaphio gold cups, with scenes of men taming wild bulls, are regarded as among the best surviving examples of Mycenaean art. They were found in a *tholos* (Mycenaean tomb shaped like a beehive) at Vaphio, near Sparta.

Cycladic Collection – Gallery 6

This room contains some of the superbly minimalist marble figurines of the 3rd and 2nd millennia BCE that inspired artists such as Picasso. One splendid example measures 1.52m and dates from 2600 to 2300 BCE.

Sounion Kouros – Gallery 8

The galleries to the left of the entrance house the oldest and most significant pieces of the sculpture collection. Galleries 7 to 13 exhibit fine examples of Archaic *kouroi* (male statues) from the 7th century BCE to 480 BCE. The most dazzling by far is the colossal 600 BCE Sounion Kouros (gallery 8), which stood before the Temple of Poseidon at Cape Sounion. Its style marks a transition point in art history, starting with the rigid lines of older Egyptian carving but also showing some of the lifelike qualities that the Greeks would come to develop in later centuries.

★ Top Tips

○ A joint museum ticket is available for €15 (€8 for students), valid for three days here and at the neighbouring Epigraphical Museum, plus the Byzantine & Christian Museum and the Numismatic Museum.

○ Arrive early to beat the rush. If you come after tour groups, head upstairs first.

○ Allow a few hours and more if you have a special interest.

○ Entrance is free on 6 March, 18 April, 18 May, the last weekend of September, 28 October, and the first Sunday of the month from 1 November to 31 March.

✕ Take a Break

The self-service **museum cafe**, with drinks, sandwiches and cakes, is in the basement and has seating in a lovely open-air courtyard.

For a meal, head into Exarhia, to a place such as Yiantes (p138) for fresh modern Greek food with a glass of wine.

Artemision Bronze – Gallery 15

This room is dominated by the incredibly precise, just-larger-than-life 460 BCE bronze statue of Zeus or Poseidon (no one knows which), excavated from the sea off Evia in 1928. The muscled figure has an iconic bearded face and holds his arms outstretched, his right arm raised to throw what was once a lightning bolt (if Zeus) or trident (if Poseidon).

Varvakeion Athena – Gallery 20

Admire the details on this statue of Athena, made in 200 CE: the helmet topped with a sphinx and griffins, a Gorgon shield and the hand holding a small figure of winged Nike (missing its head). Now imagine it all more than 10 times larger and covered in gold – that was the legendary, now-lost colossal figure of Athena Parthenos (11.5m tall) that the master sculptor Pheidias erected in the Parthenon in the 5th century BCE.

Jockey of Artemision – Gallery 21

This is another find from the shipwreck off Evia excavated in 1928. This delicately rendered bronze horse and rider dates from the 2nd century BCE; only a few parts were found at first, and it was reassembled in 1972.

Antikythera Shipwreck – Galleries 28 and 38

Treasures discovered in 1900 by sponge divers off the island of Antikythera (gallery 28) include the striking bronze **Antikythera Youth**, from the 4th century BCE. His hand once held some spherical object. More magical still is the **Antikythera Mechanism** (gallery 38), an elaborate geared device, now in fragments.

Egyptian Galleries – Galleries 40 and 41

This two-room gallery presents the best of the museum's significant Egyptian collection, the only one in Greece. Dating from 5000 BCE to the Roman conquest, artefacts include mummies, bronze figurines and beautifully evocative Roman-era painted portraits from caskets.

Akrotiri Frescoes – Gallery 48

Upstairs, room 48 is devoted to the spectacular and incredibly old Minoan frescoes from a prehistoric settlement on Santorini (Thira). They were preserved by being buried by a volcanic eruption in the late 16th century BCE.

Panathenaic Amphorae – Gallery 56

This room displays some of the ceramic vases presented to the winners of the Panathenaic Games. Each one contained oil from the sacred olive trees of Athens; victors might have received up to 140 of them. The vases are painted with scenes from the relevant sport (wrestling, in this case) on one side and an armed Athena Promachos (Athena as Champion) on the other.

National Archaeological Museum

1st Floor

- Pottery Collection
- Pottery Collection
- Cypriot Collection
- **Panathenaic Amphorae**
- Lift
- Thira Gallery
- **Akrotiri Frescoes**

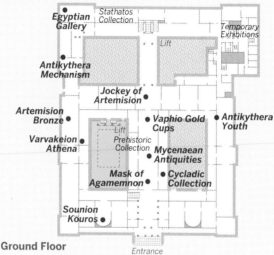

Ground Floor

- **Egyptian Gallery**
- Stathatos Collection
- Temporary Exhibitions
- Lift
- **Antikythera Mechanism**
- **Jockey of Artemision**
- **Artemision Bronze**
- **Vaphio Gold Cups**
- **Antikythera Youth**
- **Varvakeion Athena**
- Lift
- Prehistoric Collection
- **Mycenaean Antiquities**
- **Mask of Agamemnon**
- **Cycladic Collection**
- **Sounion Kouros**

Entrance

Basement

- Lift
- Toilets
- Cafe
- Museum Shop

Walking Tour 🥾

Neighbourhood Life in Exarhia

On the one hand, Exarhia is known for its anti-capitalist politics and its squatted buildings. On the other, it has loads of thriving little shops, especially for collectors' items and books, plus publishing houses. The bar scene is one of the city's most lively, distinctly casual and student-friendly, and live music lights up many a venue.

Walk Facts

Start Plateia Exarhion

Finish Emmanuel Benaki and Valtetsiou

Length 1.5km; one hour

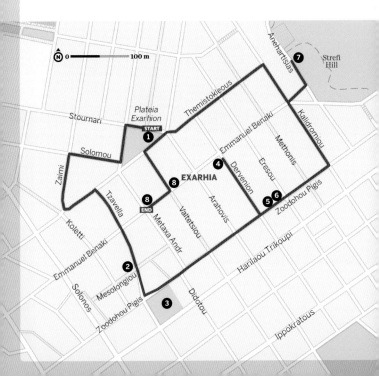

❶ Plateia Exarhion

This square (triangle, really) is the centre of neighbourhood life, and there is very often some political event taking place. Pick a spot for prime people-watching – any of the cafes on Themistokleous, or, at a slight remove but with a view downhill, **Ivi** (p143) on Stournari.

❷ Streets as Galleries

The walls, alleys and stairways of Exarhia are adorned with some of the world's most creative street art, often with a pointed underlying political message. At the corner of Mesolongiou and Tzavella is a **memorial for Alexis Grigoropoulos**, the teen whose 2008 murder by police was a political flashpoint across the country.

❸ Reclaimed Square

In 2009 the inhabitants of Exarhia claimed most of a city block, formerly a parking lot, to use as a green space. Now **Navarino Park** has a playground and vegetable patches, and it's still all planted and maintained locally, and always developing.

❹ Old-World Taverna Reborn

Lunch at **Café Boheme Barbagiannis** (p141), a jazzy, brasserie-like spot inhabiting the former Barbagiannis taverna – an Exarhia institution – with great wines and delicious, fresh Greek food. Grab a table on the sprawling sidewalk patio and watch the street life.

❺ Record Shopping

Exarhia's fun and super-niche shops include the chance to pick up, among other things, old-school vinyl. Serious music fans comb **Plan 59** (p144), for instance, for vintage psychedelia and rare Greek pressings.

❻ Spend Nothing

The secondhand shop **Skoros** (https://skoroscc.espivblogs.net) represents Exarhia's community spirit: there's no money involved. The policy is 'give what you can, take what you like.' Though it's closed in summer.

❼ Head for the Hill

Strefi Hill, up the (graffiti-bedecked) stairs on the northeast side of the neighbourhood, is where residents congregate around sundown. Have a beer at **Exostrefis** (p143).

❽ Go Cretan for Dinner

Neighbourhood denizens love **Rakoumel** (https://rakoumel.gr; 📶) and **Oxo Nou** (www.facebook.com/oxonouathens; 📶) for their super Cretan food, featuring mountain herbs and slow-cooked meats. These lively restaurants are just a block apart, so you could sample small plates at both.

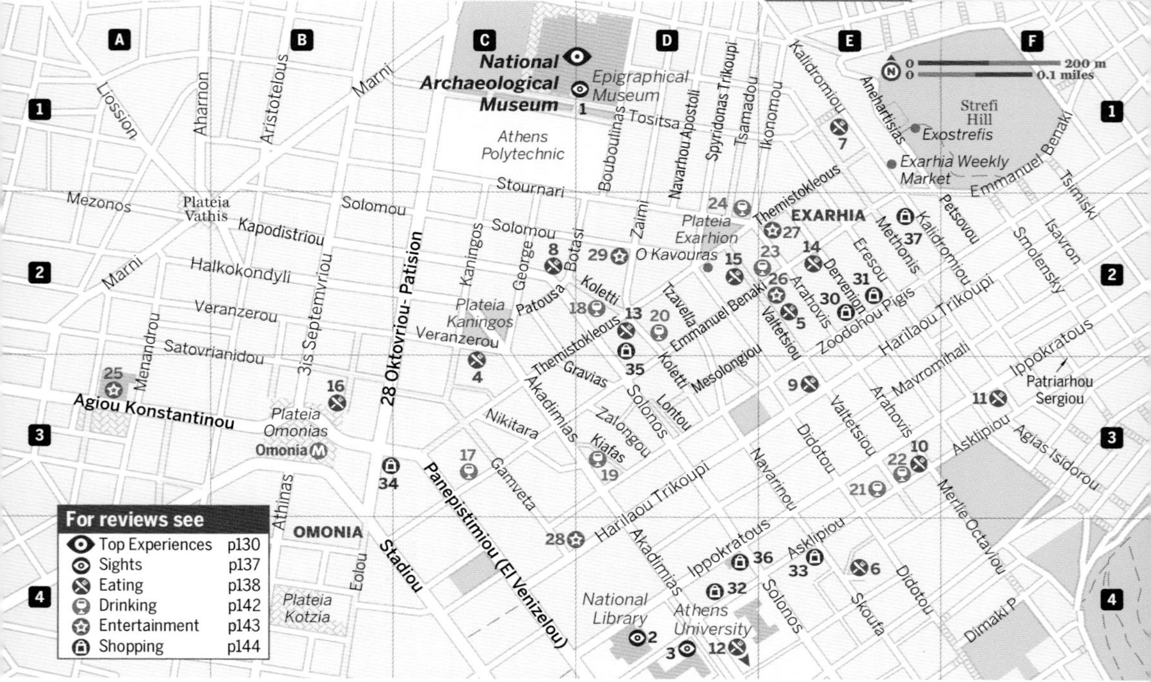

Omonia & Exarhia

EXARHIA

OMONIA

National Archaeological Museum

Athens Polytechnic

Athens University

National Library

Strefi Hill

Exarhia Weekly Market

Plateia Exarhion

Plateia Omonias

Plateia Kotzia

Plateia Vathis

Plate

For reviews see
- Top Experiences p130
- Sights p137
- Eating p138
- Drinking p142
- Entertainment p143
- Shopping p144

0   200 m
0   0.1 miles

Panepistimiou (El Venizelou)

28 Oktovriou-Patision

Agiou Konstantinou

Sights

Epigraphical Museum   MUSEUM

1 MAP P136, D1

On the south side of the National Archaeological Museum, this is an important collection of Greek inscriptions, but the main halls' tersely labelled shelves of stones are uninspiring to the casual visitor. Two newer sections, however, give some background on the Greek writing system and show off the most historically revealing pieces, such as a 3rd-century copy (or perhaps forgery) of the decree ordering the evacuation of Athens before the 480 BCE Persian invasion.

To decode some of the writing yourself, ask the staff for a sheet of ancient alphabet variations. (http://odysseus.culture.gr)

National Library   HISTORIC BUILDING

2 MAP P136, D4

One of the neoclassical 'trilogy' of buildings on Panepistimiu, the late-19th-century National Library is a dazzling design by Danish architect Theophil Hansen. Serious academic researchers can gain access to the amazing interior; otherwise, visiting here is restricted to a quick peep in the entry hall and a photo op on the grand sweeping staircase. (www.nlg.gr)

Athens University   UNIVERSITY

3 MAP P136, D4

This splendid building was designed by Danish architect

National Library

Christian Hansen and completed in 1864. The university has expanded massively around the city (enrolment is more than 100,000 students), and Hansen's building still serves as the university's administrative headquarters and ceremonial hall.

Adjacent to the south is the more ornate Athens Academy, modelled on Plato's Academy and still Greece's most prestigious research institution. Admire the two school buildings' neoclassical facades from the street; neither is open to the public. (www.uoa.gr)

Eating

I Kriti
CRETAN €€

5 ❌ MAP P136, C3

There is no shortage of Cretan restaurants in Athens, but this is the one that Cretans themselves recommend, especially for rare seasonal treats such as stewed snails, bittersweet pickled *volvi* (wild bulbs), and tender baby goat with nuts and garlic. It occupies several storefronts inside the arcade; on weekends it's a good idea to reserve. (📞)

Yiantes
TAVERNA €€

5 ❌ MAP P136, E2

This lovely restaurant with a central courtyard garden is upmarket for Exarhia and the food is superb, made with largely organic produce. Expect interesting seasonal greens such as *almirikia* (sea beans), perfectly grilled fish or delicious seasoning and herbs on meats and shellfish. (www.facebook.com/yiantes2000; 📷)

Fine Mess Smokehouse
STEAK €€

6 ❌ MAP P136, E4

Smoked in beechwood fires all day long, the meats here are packed with succulent flavour. From short ribs to brisket and even 'Thanksgiving turkey', recipes are inspired by American culinary traditions. For the non-meat eaters there's usually a pasta on the menu and quinoa and vegetable salads, plus rich desserts. (www.finemess.gr)

Ama Lachei stis Nefelis
GREEK €

7 ❌ MAP P136, E1

This modern *mezedhopoleio* (restaurant specialising in mezedhes) is a minor hike up Exarhia's hill, but you're rewarded with a lovely setting – an old school building, with tables outside in the vine-shaded playground – and super-savoury small plates that go well with drinks. Think pickled octopus, meatballs flavoured with cinnamon and cloves, and lamb kebabs. (https://restaurant-47828.business.site)

Atitamos
MEZEDHES €

8 ❌ MAP P136, C2

Cheap and cheerful, this streetside *mezedhopoleio* serves fresh, delicious small plates, from moussaka to dolmadhes (vine-leaf wraps).

Exarhia's Political Legacy

Exarhia's anarchic reputation developed in the dark years of Greece's military junta. The neighbourhood was freshly galvanised by a brutal killing by police in 2008. And in 2022 protests took place over the building of a metro station in Exarhia's central square, fenced off and guarded by riot police.

The Athens Polytechnic Uprising

On 21 April 1967 a group of army colonels staged a coup and installed Georgios Papadopoulos, as prime minister. The regime declared martial law, banned political parties and trade unions, imposed censorship and imprisoned and tortured thousands of dissidents. Others, including actress and activist Melina Mercouri, were exiled.

In 1973 students began striking in protest. On 14 November students at Athens Polytechnic – the university immediately south of the archaeological museum – began a sit-in, broadcasting a call for an uprising over their pirate radio station. Three days later, the military sent a tank crashing in. No university students died, but scores of others (the number is still disputed, anywhere from 24 to 40) were killed at companion protests, and hundreds were injured.

In the backlash, token 'liberalisation' was halted and an even-harder-line general staged a second coup. But in 1974 the dictatorship collapsed in chaos after Turkey invaded Cyprus. Behind the university's front gates, a large bronze head stands as a memorial to those killed.

The Killing of Alexis Grigoropoulos

In 2008, 15-year-old Alexis Grigoropoulos was shot dead by police in Exarhia. The police claimed the teen was an anarchist troublemaker, but eyewitnesses said the kid – who was from a rich suburb of Athens – had only been hanging out with friends.

Greeks were already angry, as Greece's debt crisis was just coming to light, and the conservative government had pushed through unpopular pension cuts and privatisation. Hours after Grigoropoulos' death, Exarhia was teeming with rioters. Demonstrations spread across the country and lasted the rest of the month. This did nothing to halt any of the cutbacks.

Exarhia commemorates the Athens Polytechnic uprising (17 November, now a national holiday) and Grigoropoulos' death (6 December) with chaotic demonstrations. It's wise to steer clear on these days; tear gas isn't uncommon.

Moussaka with egg plant

Save room for honey-dripping baklava. (www.facebook.com/atitamos)

Kimatothrafstis

TAVERNA €

9 MAP P136, E3

This great-value, bright and casual little cafe dishes out a range of homestyle Greek cooking and alternative fare. Choose from the day's offerings at the cafeteria-style display. Plates come in two sizes: large, with a choice of seven items, or small, with a choice of four. (📶 ✏️)

Ipovrihio

GREEK €

10 MAP P136, E3

The 'Submarine' is a typical Exarhia hang-out, colourful and cramped. Raki is encouraged, and the booze is offset by a big range of home-cooked Greek standards (pork chops, Cretan rusk salads, lots of veg options) and pastas that meet Italian standards of toothiness. Food comes in 'small' portions, great for solo diners or tasting a range of things.

Hayat

TURKISH €

11 MAP P136, F3

Hayat's Kurdish eats are hearty and well spiced, from the deceptively simple lentil soup to good-value kebabs and stews, all served with delish chewy bread. Also ideal for quick snacks. (www.facebook.com/Hayatgeuseis)

Piadina Lumbro

PIZZA €

12 MAP P136, D4

Simple and delicious, pizzas made from scratch and hand-held wraps based on piadina, a round flatbread from Emilia Romagna. Round out your meal with panna cotta and other Italian sweet treats. (www.piadinalumbro.gr)

Doureios Ippos

TAVERNA €

13 MAP P136, D2

In summer this family-run taverna can look abandoned – but that's because everyone is up on the roof terrace, shaded by the climbing vines.

Meaning 'Trojan Horse', it's been in business since 1965, relatively unchanged, and cooks all its meat over a charcoal fire. (www.facebook.com/doureiosippos.athens)

Café Boheme Barbagiannis

CAFE €

14 MAP P136, E2

This jazzy, brasserie-like spot in the former Barbagiannis taverna – an Exarhia institution since 1915 – is good for both a quiet coffee during the day and for a more lively evening of drinking great wines and sampling delicious, fresh Greek food. (http://cafeboheme.gr)

Rozalia

TAVERNA €€

15 MAP P136, D2

An Exarhia favourite on a lively pedestrian strip, this family-run taverna serves grills and home-style fare.

Mezedhes are brought around on a tray, so you can point and pick. Pavement tables are tempting, but better yet, sit in the garden. (www.rozalia.gr)

Veneti

CAFE €

16 MAP P136, B3

Legendary cafe Neon, famous haunt of Athens literati, fell victim to the crisis.

But the expansive space got a solid new tenant in local chain Veneti (aka Beneth, if you read the Greek letters in English), which has filled the lower level with quality pastries, cookies, pies and even hot meals.

Alexandrino (p143)

VANGELIS KORONAKIS/LONELY PLANET ©

There's seating upstairs and out on the square. (www.fournos-veneti.gr)

Drinking

Taf Coffee
COFFEE

17 MAP P136, C3

One of the best of Athens' third-wave coffee roasters, with distribution around the country and a bit abroad. Sip a pour-over here, or grab a quick espresso at the front bar. A nice touch are tasting notes (in English) of the daily coffee blends. (www.cafetaf.gr)

Revolt
BAR

18 MAP P136, D2

This small, simple bar with tables spilling out onto a pedestrian street anchors a few solid blocks of lively nightlife. The vibrant murals out front are super. Start here and explore down Koletti as far as Mesolongiou and the pedestrian blocks there. (www.facebook.com/Revoltstreetbar)

Tsin Tsin
BAR

19 MAP P136, D3

Teeny, tiny and a bit out of the way on a little lane. The bartender knows the craft and the loungey feel is relaxing. (www.facebook.com/tsintsinathens)

Beatniks Road Bar
BAR

20 MAP P136, D2

Casual and friendly, this bar offers a good list of beers on tap, cocktails and occasional DJs and live music with a leaning towards blues and rock-n-roll.

The owners are usually on hand and happy to strike up a conversation.

Nabokov
BAR

21 MAP P136, E3

Just what you expect in an Exarhia bar: literary leanings, retro music, a bit of food and customers who treat it like their lifelong haunt, even though it only opened in 2017.

There's even a pinball machine squashed in the corner.

Tralala
BAR

22 MAP P136, E3

A creative set frequents quirky Tralala, with its glitter balls, original artwork, lively owners, gregarious

Saturday Street Market

With rowdy traders working against lovely neoclassical buildings, Exarhia's **laïki agora** (Exarhia Weekly Market; Map p136, E1) – the market that takes over a street in each big neighbourhood one day a week – is especially good. Visitors won't have much practical use for the produce and household goods, but look for the roving ouzo seller. Or camp at a cafe and spectate.

atmosphere and music to match. (www.facebook.com/TralalaCafe)

Alexandrino   COCKTAIL BAR

23 MAP P136, E2

This bar, with the look of a cute, tiny French bistro, serves excellent wines and cocktails. Closed August.

Ivi   COFFEE

24 MAP P136, D2

There are plenty of options for a freddo espresso right around Exarhia's main square, but this place is extra-pleasant due to its breezy open front and chill music. It attracts local creatives working on laptops and brainstorming together. ()

Entertainment

National Theatre   THEATRE

25 MAP P136, A3

One of the city's finest neoclassical buildings hosts contemporary theatre and ancient plays.

The organisation also supports performances in other venues around town and, in summer, in ancient theatres across Greece.

Happily for tourists, some of the productions are surtitled in English, and tickets are reasonably priced. (www.n-t.gr)

Riviera   CINEMA

26 MAP P136, E2

Screening since 1969, the outdoor cinema Riviera tends towards

Exarhia's Sundown Spot

Climb any hill in Greece, and there's usually a cafe. The one on Strefi Hill, **Exostrefis** (Map p136, E1), is a casual place for a coffee or afternoon beer and small snacks, alongside neighbourhood regulars who come up to enjoy the sunset. There's live music weekend evenings (minimum charge €10). In winter, the 'downstairs' location – a restaurant in a basement on Plateia Exarhion – is livelier.

art-house programming, with new indie films and occasional programs of artists' shorts and other one-offs. (www.facebook.com/riviera.athens)

Vox   CINEMA

27 MAP P136, E2

Vox open-air cinema on Exarhia's main square has been around since 1938, and fortunately has received historic-building designation. Still, it has the rough-and-ready vibe you'd expect in this neighbourhood. Arrive early and have a drink at the ground-floor cafe. (www.facebook.com/vox.athens)

Feidiou 2 Music Cafe   LIVE MUSIC

28 MAP P136, D4

Traditional music, usually *rembetika* (blues-type songs) and other heartfelt tunes, starts around

Rembetika Revival

○ Athens' thriving music scene includes a powerful *rembetika* (bluesy songs from the early 20th century) tradition, and Exarhia is a great place to sample this soulful musical style.

○ One of Athens' longest-running *rembetika* haunts is **O Kavouras** (Map p136, D2), where the party goes till dawn (winters only, though; in general, indoor-only venues close in summer).

○ Also check smaller bars in the neighbourhood, on Emmanuel Benaki and an especially lively strip, very popular with students, around the intersection of Koletti and Mesolongiou.

10pm most nights, at this cosy little space on the edge of Exarhia. Attracts a nice mixed crowd of all ages. (www.facebook.com/Feidiou2)

AN Club   LIVE MUSIC

29 ⭐ MAP P136, D2

A small spot with a long history of live rock, featuring lesser-known international and local bands, especially metal. (www.anclub.gr)

Shopping

Zacharias   FASHION & ACCESSORIES

30 🔒 MAP P136, E2

This Greek-Spanish duo specialises in silkscreen designs inspired by classical motifs. Especially nice are their leather notebooks, wallets and more, where black ink on the natural hide echoes the colours of ancient pottery. Some of their work features in museum shops, but this storefront and workspace has the best selection. (www.zacharias.es)

Plan 59   MUSIC

31 🔒 MAP P136, E2

Between this and Old School Records next door, your vintage vinyl needs are covered. Both stock a lot of jazz and psychedelia, while Plan 59 has more Greek music as well as books and magazines. (http://plan59.wordpress.com)

Politeia   BOOKS

32 🔒 MAP P136, D4

This large bookshop occupying four storefronts stocks plenty of English-language books, filed in the relevant sections. And because it's on the edge of Exarhia, it's brimming with political theory books. (www.politeianet.gr)

Koukoutsi   FASHION & ACCESSORIES

33 🔒 MAP P136, E4

Niko and Taso design the simple, elegant Athens- and Greece-inspired graphics that adorn the T-shirts, accessories and art prints sold in this tiny shop. Their products are available in a few other boutiques and gift shops around the city, but this one has the largest selection in a full range of sizes and colours. (www.koukoutsi.net)

Loumidi COFFEE

34 🔒 MAP P136, B3

From 1920, the Loumidis family built Greece's famous Papagalo coffee brand, now owned by an international conglomerate. The original shop lives on; a pretty little jewel-box version of the typical nuts-candy-coffee-tea store that's a cornerstone of every Athens neighbourhood. (www.kafekopteialoumidi.gr)

Comicon Shop COMICS

35 🔒 MAP P136, D2

Browse a full range of Greek indie comics, graphic novels and zines. (www.comicon-shop.gr)

Travel Bookstore BOOKS

36 🔒 MAP P136, D4

Good central place for maps and guides. (www.travelbookstore.gr)

Ellinika Kouloudia FOOD & DRINKS

37 🔒 MAP P136, E2

Right in the thick of Saturday's lively street market, this quaint deli has a delectable array of traditional products, such as honey, cheese and herbs, as well as wine and ouzo.

National Theatre (p143)

Explore

Filopappou Hill, Thisio & Petralona

Escape the hectic parts of Athens by chilling out at a quiet cafe or taking a stroll and finding yourself alone among lizards and ancient stones. Filopappou and its neighbouring hills offer welcome green space, and the neighbourhoods of Thisio and Petralona are a short walk nearby, but a world away from the tourist drag.

The Short List

○ **Hill of the Pnyx (p151)** Making a pilgrimage to the site of the first formal democratic assemblies.

○ **Church of Agios Dimitrios Loumbardiaris (p149)** Lighting a candle in this exceptionally atmospheric Byzantine church.

○ **Cafe life (p153)** Enjoying a coffee or ouzo and watching the world go by at a cafe-bar on the area's pedestrianised streets.

○ **Dora Stratou Dance Theatre (p155)** Seeing Greek folk heritage on display at this regional dance theatre.

○ **Shrine of the Muses (p149)** Leaving an offering at this niche in Filopappou Hill, which has been an inspiration to artists for millennia.

Getting There & Around

Ⓜ Thissio station (green line) and walk up pedestrianised Apostolou Pavlou.

Ⓜ Akropoli station (red line) and walk west on Dionysiou Areopagitou.

Ⓜ Petralona (green line) looks convenient, but due to the hill it can be easier to walk from Thisio.

Filopappou Hill, Thisio & Petralona Map on p150

Top Experience
Stroll Up Filopappou Hill

Also called the Hill of the Muses, Filopappou Hill   ◉ MAP P150, D6
– along with the Hills of the Pnyx and Nymphs
(p151) – was, according to Plutarch, where
Theseus and the Amazons did battle. Today the
pine-clad slopes are a relaxing place for a stroll,
plus an excellent vantage point for photographing
the Acropolis. There are also a few notable ruins.

Church of Agios Dimitrios Loumbardiaris

This 16th-century **church** (www.facebook.com/agiosdimitriosloumpardiaris) may not be the oldest in Athens, but it is certainly one of the loveliest, with a timber roof, marble floors and a permanent scent of incense. A great 1732 fresco of St Dimitrios astride his horse adorns the interior.

In 1648, the church was the site of a reported miracle. The Turks, ensconced on the Acropolis, prepared to fire a cannon on worshippers in the church, but the gunner was killed by lightning, saving the congregation. Hence its name, Loumbardiaris ('of the cannon').

Socrates' Prison

Enter the cover of pines, with doves cooing, and follow the path to this warren of rooms carved into bedrock; it's said to have been the place where Socrates was imprisoned prior to his trial in 399 BCE. During WWII artefacts from the Acropolis and National Archaeological Museum were hidden here to protect them from looting.

Shrine of the Muses & Fortifications

Up the marble-cobbled stairs – designed by architect Dimitris Pikionis, each stone placed just so – you reach a niche in the bedrock, a **shrine** dedicated to the goddesses of creative inspiration. Even today, grateful or hopeful artists place offerings on a small stone cairn. Ruins of 4th- and 5th-century-BCE **defensive walls** criss-cross the hill.

Monument of Filopappos

This 12m-high marble monument marks the summit of the hill. It was built between 114 and 116 CE in honour of Julius Antiochus Filopappos, a Roman consul and administrator. The top middle niche depicts Filopappos enthroned; the bottom frieze shows him in a chariot with his entourage.

★ Top Tips

○ Small footpaths weave all over the hill, but the paved path to the top starts near the *periptero* (kiosk) on Dionysiou Areopagitou.

○ The summit gives one of the best views of the Acropolis and Attica – sunset and early evening offer spectacular light.

○ The hilltop above the treeline is exposed: bring sunscreen, a hat and water, and rain gear on wet days.

○ English-language placards placed at major features explain the rich ancient history of the hill.

✕ Take a Break

For refreshment, drop down to the cafes in Thisio, either on the main pedestrian route or back on Iraklidon. Akropol (p153) is in the thick of the action.

Otherwise, have a full meal at a restaurant such as Merceri Food & Drink (p152).

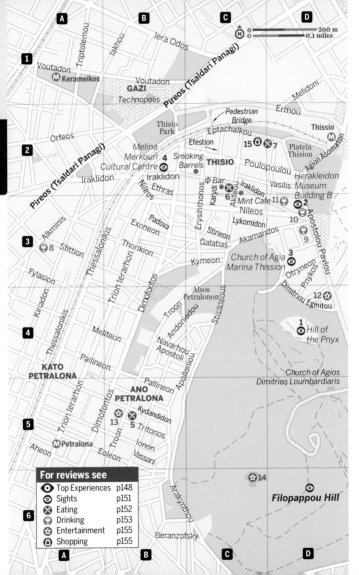

A | B | C | D

0 ——— 200 m
0 ——— 0.1 miles

1
Voutadon
Triptolemou
Iakhou
Iera Odos
Melidoni

Ⓜ Kerameikos
Voutadon
GAZI
Pireos (Tsaldari Panagi)
Ermou

Technopolis
Ermou
Thissio
Ⓜ

Orfeos
Thisio Park
Pedestrian Bridge
Eptachalkou
Plateia Thissiou
Agion Asomaton

2
Melina Merkouri Cultural Centre ◉ **4**
Efestion
15 🔒 🗡 7
Herakleidon Museum Building B

Pireos (Tsaldari Panagi)
Iraklidon
Smoking Barrels
THISIO
Poulopoulou
Vasilis

Iraklidon
Nileos
Ethras
Φ Bar
Karydi
Iraklidon
Mint Cafe 11 🍴
◉ **2**

Padova
Erysithonos
6 🗡 Akteou
Nileos
10

Exoneon
Lykomidon
Akamandos
🔒 **9**
Apostolou Pavlou

3
🍴 **8**
Alkminis
Thessalonikis
Thorikion
Stirieon
Galatias
Church of Agia Marina Thission
◉ **3**
Otryneon
Pnykos

Sfittion
Dimfontos
Kymeon
Alsos Petralonon
Dimitriou Eginitou
🌟 **12**

Fylasion
Kiriadon
Trion Ierarhon
Troon
Andonadou
Stisikleous
Ⓘ **1** Hill of the Pnyx

4
Meliteon
Navarhou Apostoli
Church of Agios Dimitrios Loumbardiaris

Thessalonikis
Pallineon
KATO PETRALONA

Trion Ierarhon
Pallineon
Apolloniou
ANO PETRALONA

5
Dimfontos
Kydandidon
🌟 **13**
🗡 **5** Tritonos
Ⓜ Petralona
Troon
Ionon
Vassani

Aheon
Eoleon

🌟 **14**
Filopappou Hill

6

Beranzofsky
Arakynthou

For reviews see
◉ Top Experiences   p148
◉ Sights   p151
🗡 Eating   p152
🍴 Drinking   p153
🌟 Entertainment   p155
🔒 Shopping   p155

A | B | C | D

Sights

Hill of the Pnyx

PARK

1 ⊙ MAP P150, D4

North of Filopappou Hill (p148), this hill was the official meeting place of the Democratic Assembly in the 5th century BCE – really, the first site of democracy. You can see the speakers' steps, where the great orators Aristides, Demosthenes, Pericles and Themistocles addressed assemblies. (More recently, politicians have used it for photo ops.) The hill is often empty, save for birds, and its view of the Acropolis' front steps gives a real sense of the temples' centrality to ancient Athenian life. To the northwest is the **Hill of the Nymphs**, topped with the old Athens observatory, built in 1842.

Herakleidon Museum Building B

MUSEUM

2 ⊙ MAP P150, D3

This eclectic museum, split over two locations, examines the interrelation of art, mathematics and philosophy, explored through rotating exhibits on such diverse subjects as ancient robotic and computer technology, and shipbuilding. Building B focuses on weapons of war, including triremes, the ancient warships that allowed the Greeks to conquer the Persians at the Battle of Salamis.

Around the corner in a restored mansion, the smaller **Building A** (www.herakleidon-art.gr) has an exhibition on automata, featuring an ancient type of robot. The museum also holds one of the world's biggest collections of MC Escher artworks

Hill of the Pnyx

APOSTOLIS GIONTZIS/SHUTTERSTOCK ©

(though it is not always on view). (www.herakleidon-gr.org)

Church of Agia Marina Thission

CHURCH

3 MAP P150, D3

Striped like a multilayered cake and bursting with red-tile domes, this 1931 church perches on the northwest side of the Hill of the Nymphs. Its murals, with a whiff of art nouveau, are lovely. Look inside for the much smaller chapel in the southeast corner, carved directly into the bedrock. It dates to the 11th or 12th century and has long been a site for health and fertility rituals.

Melina Merkouri Cultural Centre

MUSEUM

4 ⊙ MAP P150, B2

For anyone who loves the Greek tradition of *karagiozi* (shadow puppets), this free museum is a treat, packed with the creations of master puppeteer Haridimos (Sotiris Haritos). There's very little English signage,

---

Country in the City

In Ano Petralona, on Kallisthenous around Aristragora, the street is lined with small, village-style stone cottages. They were built in the mid-20th century as workers' housing by the architect Dimitris Pikionis, who also designed the paths on Filopappou Hill.

---

but the displays tell their own stories. Upstairs is a mock street scene of 'old Athens', with shop windows of the typesetter, the photo studio, the barber and more. Call ahead to see if they have a puppet show – there's often one at 11am on Sunday. (www.cityofathens.gr/node/676)

Eating

Oikonomou

TAVERNA €€

5 MAP P150, B5

As traditional, no-frills neighbourhood tavernas are slowly disappearing, it's worth making a trip to this stalwart, which excels in homestyle stews cooked with care. (It's also a good reason to visit this nice neighbourhood.) The best way to decide what to eat is to visit the kitchen and peek into the day's array of pots.

Merceri Food & Drink

MEDITERRANEAN €€

6 ✖ MAP P150, C2

Drawing inspiration from across the Med and using seasonal ingredients, the two chefs – Maria Dioudi and Melina Chomata – create modern, delicate flavour combinations from tuna tartare with honey, anise and ginger to rib-eye steak with asparagus and shiitaki mushrooms. The excellent wine list is a delight, too. (www.merceri.gr)

Steki tou Ilia

TAVERNA €€

7 ✖ MAP P150, D2

If there's a queue to dine at this popular *psistaria* (restaurant serving

Early Greek Philosophers

Late-5th- and early-4th-century-BCE philosophers introduced new modes of thought rooted in rationality, logic and reason: gifts that have shaped Western philosophy ever since. These are the big names:

Socrates (469–399 BCE) Athens' most noble citizen taught his students to reason for themselves by asking probing questions. He was charged with corrupting the city's youth, then jailed (on Filopappou Hill, according to legend) and sentenced to death by drinking hemlock. His legacy is a mode of reason based on eliminating hypotheses through questions – the so-called Socratic method.

Plato (427–347 BCE) Socrates' star student documented his teacher's thoughts in books such as the *Symposium*. Plato wrote *The Republic* to warn Athens that unless its people respected law and leadership, and educated its youth, it would be doomed.

Aristotle (384–322 BCE) Plato's student established his own school (p109) and worked in fields such as astronomy, physics, zoology, ethics and politics. Aristotle was also the personal physician to Philip II, King of Macedon, and tutor of Alexander the Great.

---

grilled food), it's worth joining. The payoff is succulent lamb and pork, barrel wine and dips, chips and salads. In summer, it moves across the street into a hidden garden. (www.facebook.com/tostekitouilia)

Drinking

Upopa Epops   BAR

 8 MAP P150, A3

This lovely bar-restaurant is one of the reasons Petralona is considered a just-the-right-amount-of-cool neighbourhood. It has numerous rooms filled with vintage furniture and a pretty courtyard, the food and drinks are great and there's often a DJ, but there's always a place to have a conversation. (www.facebook.com/upupaepopsthebar2016)

Akropol   CAFE

9 MAP P150, D3

This 'vintage cafe' is only a few years old but has put some effort into looking and feeling like it's been around for decades. It has music nights that draw neighbours as well as curious tourists. (www.acropolvintage.gr)

Sin Athina   CAFE

10 MAP P150, D3

Location, location, location! This cafe-bar sits at the junction of the two pedestrianised strips and has a sweeping view up to the Acropolis.

The Ancient Greek Pantheon

Ancient Greek religion honoured the '12 Olympians', the immortals who dwelt on Mt Olympus, as well as other gods, goddesses and demigods, all known to meddle or intervene in human affairs. Each city-state had a patron, and people made personal appeals too.

Greek Gods and Goddesses: Who's Who

Zeus (Roman name: Jupiter) Thunderbolt-flinging king of Mt Olympus and master of disguise in pursuit of mortal maidens.

Hera (Juno) Protector of women and family, the queen of heaven is both the wife and sister of Zeus. In myths, she often takes revenge on Zeus' illegitimate children.

Poseidon (Neptune) God of the seas, master of the mists and younger brother of Zeus. He dwells in an underwater palace.

Athena (Minerva) Goddess of wisdom, war and science and guardian of Athens, born in full armour out of Zeus' forehead. Diplomatic in war.

Ares (Mars) God of war. Unlike Athena, bloodthirsty and lacking control. Patron of Sparta, not coincidentally.

Aphrodite (Venus) Goddess of love and beauty, born of sea foam. Son and helper: cherubic Eros (Cupid).

Hephaestus (Vulcan) God of craftsmanship, metallurgy and fire. He punished man with a woman, Pandora (with her box of evils).

Apollo God of philosophy, arts and medicine, Apollo was also the god of the sun and an expert shot with a bow and arrow.

Artemis (Diana) Goddess of the hunt and twin sister of Apollo. Closely associated with Hecate, patroness of witchcraft.

Hermes (Mercury) The gods' messenger; patron of travel and trade.

Dionysos (Bacchus) Rowdy god of wine and theatre. Protector of outcasts and seeker of ecstasy.

Demeter (Ceres) Goddess of agriculture, fertility and the seasons.

Hestia (Vesta) Virgin goddess of the hearth and home.

Hades (Pluto) God of death. With the help of his skeletal ferryman, Charon, he brings the dead to the underworld.

The real magic is on the rooftop – though the menu is higher priced. (www.sinathina.gr)

The Underdog
COFFEE

11 MAP P150, D3

Far from underdogs, the championship-winning baristas here know how to make a decent cup of coffee. This speciality roaster and cafe-bar occupies a roomy location with a shaded courtyard. It also serves craft beers. (www.underdog.gr;)

Entertainment

Thission
CINEMA

12 ⭐ MAP P150, D4

Across from the Acropolis, this is a lovely old-style outdoor cinema in a garden setting. Sit towards the back if you want to catch a glimpse of the glowing edifice. Tickets are cheaper Monday to Wednesday. (www.cine-thisio.gr)

Zefiros
CINEMA

13 ⭐ MAP P150, B5

The cinephile's outdoor cinema, running obscure international films (sometimes a tricky subtitle situation) and black-and-white favourites. (http://newstarartcinema.gr/zephyros)

Dora Stratou Dance Theatre
DANCE

14 ⭐ MAP P150, C6

Every summer this company of 75 singers and dancers performs Greek folk dances, showing off the

---

Best Hang-outs

Slide into Thisio life down the refurbished train tracks, now the pedestrianised walk Iraklidon. **Mint Cafe** (Map p150, C2; www.facebook.com/mint.cafe.thissio) hooks you up with coffee, while **Φ Bar** (F Bar; Map p150, C2; www.facebook.com/rockbarathens) and **Smoking Barrels** (Map p150, C2; www.facebook.com/SmokingBarrelsAthens) lay on great cocktails. Feeling pup-deprived? Visit Filopappou and Pnyx in the evening, when residents are out walking their dogs. Petralona's *laïki agora* (produce market) takes place on Fridays. .

---

rich variety of regional costume and musical traditions. (www.grdance.org)

Shopping

Bernier/Eliades
ART

15 🔒 MAP P160, C2

This gallery, established in 1977 and occupying this grand old home since 1999, showcases prominent Greek artists and an impressive list of international artists, from abstract American impressionists to British pop.

Shows change roughly every six weeks and tend towards the minimalistic. (www.bernier-eliades.gr)

Explore ⊛

Gazi, Keramikos & Metaxourgio

Gazi's is a typical urban tale: abandoned industrial district is revived by artists and bar owners. A decade later, it's in nearby Keramikos and rough-and-tumble Metaxourgio where scruffy-cool bars and cafes are popping up, alongside derelict blocks of mansions and Chinese wholesalers.

The Short List

○ **Keramikos (p158)** *Paying respects among beautifully carved grave markers, and strolling the wildflower-covered ruins of Athens' old city gates.*

○ **Museum of Islamic Art (p163)** *Gazing on the treasures of shahs and sheikhs from centuries past.*

○ **Industrial Gas Museum (p165)** *Marvelling at the 19th-century complex of furnaces and industrial buildings like giant art installations.*

○ **Benaki Museum at 138 Pireos Street (p163)** *Learning about Greece of the 20th and 21st centuries via eclectic, ever-changing art.*

○ **Offbeat performances (p169)** *Stumbling upon a dance show in a train car at Treno sto Rouf, for instance, or experimental theatre.*

Getting There & Around

Ⓜ Kerameikos (blue line) pops up in the centre of Gazi.

Ⓜ Thissio (green line) is actually closer to the Kerameikos archaeological site.

🚗 Taxis wait in central Gazi, or you can call one. Night rates ('2' on the meter, 60% higher) kick in after midnight.

Gazi, Keramikos & Metaxourgio Map on p162

Top Experience 📷

Wander the Ruins at Kerameikos

This lush, tranquil site, uncovered in 1861 during the construction of Pireos St, is named for the potters who settled it around 3000 BCE, then on the clay-rich banks of the Iridanos River. But it's better known as a cemetery, used through the 6th century CE; the vividly carved grave markers give a sense of ancient life.

◎ MAP P162, D3

✆ 210 346 3552

http://odysseus.culture.gr

adult/child incl museum €8/free

🕐 8am-8pm, reduced hours in low season

Ⓜ Thissio

Archaeological Museum

The small but excellent **museum** contains remarkable *stelae* (grave markers) and sculptures from the site, such as the amazing 4th-century-BCE **marble bull** from the plot of Dionysos of Kollytos, as well as funerary offerings and ancient toys. Outside, don't miss the lifelike stone mountain dog.

Sacred Gate

This gate, of which only foundations remain, was where pilgrims from Eleusis entered the city during the annual Eleusinian Procession. The gate marked the end of the **Sacred Way**, aka Iera Odos, which is now a wide city street that still follows a straight route west to modern Elefsina.

Dipylon Gate

The once-massive Dipylon Gate was the city's main entrance and where the Panathenaic Procession began. The city's prostitutes also gathered here to offer their services to travellers. From a **platform** outside the gate, Pericles gave his famous speech extolling the virtues of Athens and honouring those who died in the first year of the Peloponnesian Wars. Between the Sacred and Dipylon Gates is the foundation of the **Pompeion**, a dressing room for participants in the Panathenaic Procession.

Street of Tombs

Leading off the Sacred Way to the left as you head away from the city is this avenue reserved for the graves of Athens' elite, while ordinary citizens were buried in the bordering areas. Some surviving *stelae* are now in the on-site museum and the National Archaeological Museum. What you see here are mostly replicas, but look for poignant details.

★ **Top Tips**

○ In the middle of the site, align yourself with Iera Odos, beyond the fence to the northwest – this will help you envision the gates and other buildings around the end of this historical road.

○ There is no cafe or shop immediately close by; bring water or a bottle to refill from the tap by the museum.

○ Admission to the site and the museum is included in the Acropolis combo ticket.

✕ **Take a Break**

The best place for refreshments is in Gazi and its cafes and restaurants: A Little Taste of Home (p165) for lunch, say.

A little further, in Thisio, is Steki tou Ilia (p152), reached via a pedestrian overpass across Ermou from the Kerameikos site entrance.

Walking Tour 🚶

A Night Around Gazi

The towering pylons of Gazi's gasworks glow red at night, like a beacon to party people, and the streets beyond are chock-a-block with restaurants and bars. As Gazi has grown rowdier and more mainstream, the Keramikos area and Metaxourgio have developed their own quiet, more alternative-minded scenes – though abandoned blocks at night are not for the faint of heart or solo flyer.

Walk Facts

Start Plateia Avdi, Metaxourgio

Finish Plateon and Leonidou, Keramikos

Length 1.8km; one hour (or as long as the night takes you)

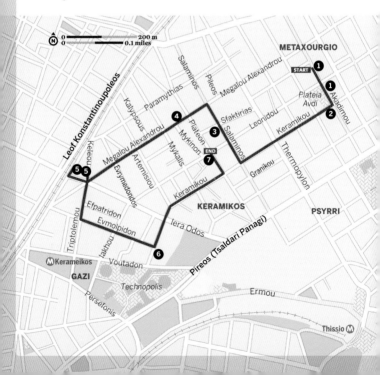

❶ First, a Cocktail

Start your evening on Plateia Avdi, where **Myrovolos** (www.facebook.com/myrovolosmetaxourgeio) is a funky lesbian-run cafe with an unrelated motorcycle club upstairs – typical Metaxourgio, in other words. There are a few other equally cool cafe-bars on the square as well, like **Blue Parrot** (p168).

❷ A Trip to the Islands

Seychelles (p166) gets packed every night; if you didn't reserve, scoot in before the 9pm dinner rush. Check the handwritten day's menu of super-fresh regional-Greek dishes in the open kitchen, or ask the tattooed chefs if they're not too busy. (The story behind the name: it's a joke about the previous business here, a coffee house named Bahamas.)

❸ Edgy Athens

After dinner, wander southeast into Keramikos, keeping your wits about you on the dodgier blocks, and find the pedestrian street of Salaminos, where **Alphaville** (www.facebook.com/seaboyathens) is just one on a strip of bohemian bars, all with a good mix of music, inexpensive drinks and loads of *kefi* (party vibes).

❹ Local Blues

Once you've laid on a couple of drinks, see if the band has started

Street Art Stroll

This area rivals Exarhia for excellent graffiti and murals, so you might want to make a separate trip in daytime. Wander on your own, or join a tour with **Alternative Athens** (p22) to learn more about the artists and the themes in their work.

at **Steki Pinoklis** (p169), a smoky taverna that usually hosts soulful classic *rembetika* (blues songs) in winter.

❺ Gay Gazi

Gazi has grown into Athens' biggest LGBTQI+ scene. One of the newer clubs on the block, **Be Queer** (p168), is super-fun and welcoming, while just around the corner, the city's long-established lesbian club **Noiz** (https://facebook.com/noizclubATH) has retro dance nights.

❻ Hot Jazz

If you're still looking for music, check who's playing at cosy **Afrikana** (p169), a little converted house that crams in jazz and African bands on a stage in the back.

❼ Late-Night Snack

A classic Athens night out ends with souvlaki, even if it's just a skewer or two. **Elvis** (p166) is the hot spot in this area, open after all the bars and almost as raucous.

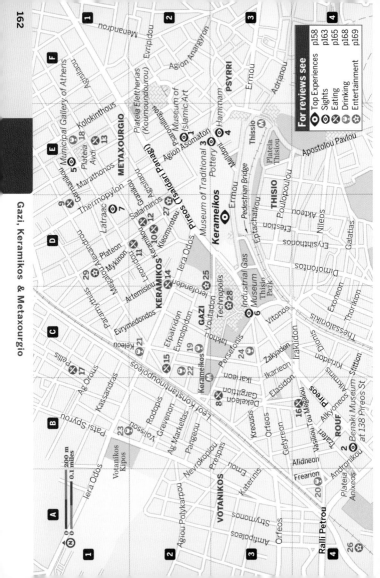

Gazi, Keramikos & Metaxourgio

For reviews see
- ◉ Top Experiences — p158
- ◉ Sights — p163
- ✕ Eating — p165
- ◇ Drinking — p168
- ◎ Entertainment — p169

Menandrou

Evripidou

Agion Anargyron

PSYRRI

Ermou

Adrianou

Ermou

Hammam

Thissio

Plateia Eleftherias
(Koumoundourou)

Museum of
Islamic Art

Agion Asomaton

Plateia
Thisiou

Apostolou Pavlou

Museum of Traditional
Pottery

Kerameikos

THISSIO

Pedestrian Bridge

Ermou

Eptachalkou

Erestion

Poulopoulou

Nileos

Akteon

Galatias

Municipal Gallery of Athens

METAXOURGIO

Kolokinthous

Plateia
Avdi

Marathonos

Thermopylon

Latrac

Salaminos

Kerameikou (Tsaldari Panagi)

Pireos

Megalou Alexandrou

Mykinon

Plateon

Leonidou

Artemisiou

Iera Odos

Keleou

Efpatridon

Evmolpidon

Evrymedondos

GAZI

Iera Odos

Iakhou

Technopolis

Industrial Gas
Museum

Thisio
Park

Vitonos

Dimortotos

Erysithonos

Exoneon

Thessalonikis

Thorikion

Voutadon

Persefonis

Zakyadon

Trakildon

Kiriadon

Dionis

Almmis

Ikarieon

Ikarion

Elasidon

Kreousis

PIREOS

Benaki Museum
at 138 Pireos St

ROUF

Vasiliou Tou Megalou

Alkyoneos

Tralen

Androniki

Plateia
Anixeos

Frearion

Ralli Petrou

200 m
0.1 miles

Sights

Museum of Islamic Art
MUSEUM

1 MAP P162, E2

While not particularly large, this museum houses a significant collection of Islamic art. Four floors of a mansion display, in ascending chronological order, exceptionally beautiful weaving, jewellery, porcelain and even a marble-floored reception room from a 17th-century Cairo mansion. Informative signage provides the detail on what you're seeing. In the basement, part of Athens' ancient Themistoklean wall is exposed. The rooftop cafe, with a great view of Keramikos, has a lovely mural:

Imagine a Palm Tree by Narvine G Khan-Dossos. (www.benaki.org)

Benaki Museum at 138 Pireos Street
MUSEUM

2 MAP P162, B4

While the main Benaki Museum of Greek Culture displays the classical and traditional, this annexe focuses on modern and inventive. Apart from a few canvases by contemporary painters that are portraits of founder Antonis Benakis, there are no permanent exhibitions here, rather several rotating temporary exhibits, which can be excellent. Also check the schedule of musical performances in its atrium courtyard. It has a pleasant cafe and an excellent gift shop. (www.benaki.org)

Museum of Islamic Art

MILAN GONDA/SHUTTERSTOCK ©

The Technopolis

Museum of
Traditional Pottery   MUSEUM

3 ◉ MAP P162, E3

If the Kerameikos site sparks your curiosity, head to this small museum around the corner. In a lovely neoclassical building, it's dedicated to the history of (relatively) contemporary Greek pottery, exhibiting a selection from the museum's collection of 4500-plus pieces. There's also a reconstruction of a traditional potter's workshop.The centre holds periodic exhibitions and there's a shop selling ceramics. (www.potterymuseum.gr)

Hammam   SPA

4 ◉ MAP P162, E3

The marble-lined steam room may be a bit small, but thanks to the attention to detail throughout, this Turkish-style place is the best of the three major bathhouses in central Athens. Amenities include proper-size water bowls, and hot tea and Turkish delight in the lounge afterwards. For the full effect, reserve ahead for a full-body scrub. (www.hammam.gr)

Municipal
Gallery of Athens   MUSEUM

5 ◉ MAP P162, E1

This city-run gallery has temporary exhibits, sometimes featuring Greek artists but not always. It's definitely worth a peek as it's set in a grand mansion that's had many incarnations, including as the silk factory for which the neighbourhood of Metaxourgio is named.

Danish architect Christian Hansen (brother of Theophil, responsible for the landmark Athens Academy building on Panepistimiou) designed it in 1833. (http://odysseus.culture.gr)

Industrial Gas Museum
NOTABLE BUILDING

6 ⊙ MAP P162, C3

It's fascinating to follow the walking route that runs through the old gasworks (p169) in Gazi, in operation from 1862 until 1984. The preserved furnaces and industrial buildings from the mid-19th century appear like giant art installations. Photos and interactive elements provide an idea of what the works were like when in operation. Head up the watchtower of the New Watergas building for a panoramic city view. The site often hosts music and other events and there's a cafe. (https://gasmuseum.gr)

Latraac
SKATE PARK

7 ⊙ MAP P162, D1

If you ever thought the problem with skateboarding was that there was nowhere to drink a coffee while you did it, Latraac has solved this for you. A wooden skate bowl occupies one half of a city lot; shaded benches for the cafe take up the other. The crowd skews adult and arty, but kids are welcome. Food is good too. (http://latraac.com)

Eating

A Little Taste of Home
INTERNATIONAL €€

8 ✗ MAP P162, B3

This successful operation was started by Ahmad, a Syrian refugee and excellent host. The concept is summed up in the name, with a range of different cultural dishes on offer – all good and fresh. It is indeed a nice homey place in the middle of the Gazi party scene. Ahmad has self-catering apartments, too. (http://alittletasteofhome.gr)

Aleria
MEDITERRANEAN €€€

9 ✗ MAP P162, D1

This contemporary, elegant restaurant in a restored mansion feels a bit surreal in the otherwise scruffy Metaxourgio neighbourhood. It does lovely, imaginative things with the freshest Greek ingredients. It also has a high-concept vegetarian tasting menu. (www.aleria.gr; 🛜 ✏)

CTC Urban Gastronomy
GASTRONOMY €€€

10 ✗ MAP P162, D2

The romantically lit courtyard is perfect for date night and the extravagant mystery of a tasting menu leads you on a culinary journey. In fact, chef Alexandros Tsiotinis has garnered a Michelin star for CTC's experimental Mediterranean cuisine. (www.ctc-restaurant.com)

Menu Advice

o Restaurants are required to post a menu outside. On long menus, only items with prices are available. When in doubt, order the day's specials.

o Upscale restaurants automatically bring bottled water, but it's fine to request tap. Bread is technically optional too. Neither is expensive, though.

o Dishes are typically served (and portioned) to share. Traditional places will sometimes do half portions for solo diners.

o Thanks to Orthodox fasting rules, traditional restaurants often have some meat-free and even vegan dishes. Best selection is during Lent, before Christmas and in summer.

o Frozen ingredients, especially seafood, are usually flagged on the menu with an asterisk.

o Fish is usually pricey, sold per kilogram and cooked whole. It is customary to go into the kitchen to select your fish (go for firm flesh and shiny eyes). Confirm the raw weight so there are no surprises on the bill.

Elvis   GREEK €

11 ⊗ MAP P162, D2

This souvlaki joint is mobbed, and not just because the counter staff slide you a shot of booze while you're waiting. The meat quality is high, the prices are right and the music is great. Every skewer comes with good chewy bread and fried potatoes. A branch in Pangrati applies the same winning formula.

Korova   GREEK €€

12 ⊗ MAP P162, D2

Busy with chatting folks quaffing beers and cocktails before tucking into excellent Greek and Mediterranean mainstays, this is Keramikos casual eating at its best. (www.facebook.com/athenskorova)

Seychelles   GREEK €€

13 ⊗ MAP P162, E1

Gutsy fresh food, an open kitchen, friendly service, a handwritten daily menu and rock on the soundtrack: Seychelles may be the Platonic ideal of a restaurant. Dishes can look simple – meaty pan-fried mushrooms with just a sliver of sheep's cheese, say, or greens with fish roe – but the flavours are excellent. Go early or book ahead; it's deservedly popular. Closed August. (www.instagram.com/seychellesrestaurant)

Bao Bao

CHINESE €

14 MAP P162, D2

Despite the many Chinese restaurants in Athens, it's hard to find one of quality. Bao Bao bucks that trend with straight-up dumplings, steamed buns (per the name) and noodle dishes that compliment a night out in Gazi. (www.baobao.gr)

Kanella

TAVERNA €€

15 MAP P162, C2

Housemade village-style bread, mismatched retro crockery and brown paper on the tabletops set the tone for this modern taverna serving regional Greek cuisine. Friendly staff offer daily specials such as lemon lamb with potatoes and an excellent zucchini and avocado salad. (www.facebook.com/kanellagazi)

Oinomperdemata

TAVERNA €

16 MAP P162, B4

Unpretentious fresh daily specials are the hallmark of this simple spot. Try staples such as fried cod with garlic dip and roast vegetables, or pork stew, rabbit and rooster. (www.oinomperdemata.gr; 🛜)

Laika

GREEK €

17 MAP P167, C1

Out on the fringes of Gazi, among car workshops and the occasional experimental theatre, this hip little cafe-bar is a treat. There's a simple but good-value food menu including dishes such as vegetarian *moussaka* (baked layers of eggplant and potatoes topped with cheese sauce) and pasta.

Grilled souvlaki

Drinking

Blue Parrot
CAFE

18 🚇 MAP P162, E1

Lashes of hanging greenery and a laid-back vibe, both inside and outside, make the Blue Parrot one of the area's most pleasant spots to hang out over a drink.

Gazarte
LIVE MUSIC BAR

19 🚇 MAP P162, C2

At this respected arts complex, hit live music with a trendy 30-something crowd. A ground-level theatre hosts live performances and the busy rooftop bar and restaurant is glorious on a summer night. Closed August. (www.gazarte.gr)

MoMix
COCKTAIL BAR

Cocktails get the molecular treatment at this bar (see 19 🚇 Map p162, c2), arriving at the table fizzing or smoking or transformed into gums and powders. In 2021 the operation moved to a fabulous new spot on the Keramikos square with a ter-

---

Theatre Scene

Black-box theatres abound in these neighbourhoods, and although most productions are in Greek, occasionally some will have English surtitles. Keep an eye out for posters. Also, **Gazarte** (p168) sometimes hosts English comedy shows.

---

race featuring Gazi and Acropolis views. (www.momixbar.com)

Beaver Collective
CAFE

20 🚇 MAP P162, A4

This women-run cooperative cafe is of course lesbian-friendly, but also just generally friendly. Sunday brunch gets a good crowd and cocktails flow freely. (www.facebook.com/collectivabeaver)

BeQueer
GAY & LESBIAN

21 🚇 MAP P162, C2

This quirky, casual club brightens up Gazi's gay bar and club scene. The vibe are friendly and open, and there are occasional theme and drag nights. (www.facebook.com/bequeerathens)

A Liar Man
BAR

22 🚇 MAP P162, C2

Colourful mosaic decorations and a more hushed vibe make this Gazi alleyway hideout a pleasant antidote to other top-volume bars and clubs nearby. It closes some summers, so check ahead. (www.facebook.com/aliarmanathens)

Big
GAY

23 🚇 MAP P162, B1

Cosy hub for Athens' lively bear scene. (www.bigbar.gr)

S-Cape
GAY & LESBIAN

24 🚇 MAP P162, C3

Stays packed with the younger gay, lesbian and transgender crowd. You gotta be willing to get smoky and close. Check theme nights online. (www.facebook.com/scape.freeyourself)

Entertainment

Afrikana   JAZZ

25 ⭐ MAP P162, D2

Just out of the fray of the Gazi scene, this little bar occupies an old house, and its small stage hosts jazz and funk bands. The atmosphere is very friendly and draws a nice mixed crowd. Cover for the band is usually €5 or so, added to the price of your first drink. Closed August. (www.facebook.com/afrikana.athens)

Treno sto Rouf   ARTS CENTRE

26 ⭐ MAP P162, A4

Look for the glowing headlight on a steam locomotive behind Rouf station. Attached is a string of old train cars converted into a restaurant, bar-cafe, music club and theatre. It's a cool place to have a drink and a snack (€6 to €15) and imagine yourself on the Orient Express of old. Closed in August. (https://totrenostorouf.gr)

Bios   MULTI-MEDIA SPACE

27 ⭐ MAP P162, D2

Occupying a Bauhaus apartment building, this multilevel warren has a great rooftop bar, restaurant, basement club and tiny art-house cinema. Expect live performances, art and new-media exhibitions, or at the very least a solid DJ and fab Acropolis view. (www.bios.gr)

Blocks to Avoid

Metaxourgio earns its somewhat dodgy reputation and at night it can be downright spooky on block after block of deserted or defunct buildings. It's especially important not to stray into the pedestrian alleys east of Plateia Avdi, where there's open-air drug use, as well as two blocks of brothels. The pink 'Studio' neon signs, dotted around Gazi and Keramikos, mark brothels as well, of a more upscale sort.

Technopolis   PERFORMING ARTS

28 ⭐ MAP P162, C3

A variety of events are scheduled throughout the year at the city's old gasworks, an impressively restored 1862 complex of industrial buildings. It hosts exhibitions, concerts, festivals and events, and has a pleasant cafe. (www.technopolis-athens.com)

Steki Pinoklis   TRADITIONAL MUSIC

29 ⭐ MAP P162, D1

Although this smoky taverna opened in 2017, its musical taste and style skews much older. This is an excellent place to hear *rembetika* songs from Smyrna plus other traditional Greek music, with a band playing most nights and Sunday afternoons. Closed August. (www.facebook.com/pinoklis)

Worth a Trip 🔭

Relax on the Golden Beaches of Faliro

On a baking-hot summer day in central Athens, don't forget that the sea is only 7km south. An excursion to the waterfront all but guarantees a refreshing breeze, and it's a great opportunity to join Athenian families at leisure, whether along the waterfront promenade or at the Stavros Niarchos Park and adjacent arts centre.

Ⓜ From Syntagma, destination Faliro. It runs past Flisvos Park and continues (slowly) to near the Stavros Niarchos Center.

🚌 Faster if going directly to Stavros Niarchos Center.

🚕 A taxi to Flisvos Park costs about €14.

Flisvos Park

The highly family-friendly **Flisvos Park** (https://parkoflisvos.gr 👼) has loads of playground facilities, an open-air cinema and the wonderful summer-only shadow-puppet theatre,

Theatro Skion Tasou Konsta (www.fkt.gr). This is a lively place around sundown, as locals come out for a *volta* (stroll) along the promenade.

Stavros Niarchos Foundation Cultural Center

The vast **Stavros Niarchos Foundation Cultural Center** (www.snfcc.org) spreads its winged roof on a hill above Faliron Bay.

Architecture buffs will love the Renzo Piano building, and readers can admire the National Library installed in one wing.

Check the schedule for arts events by the grand pool and at the **Greek National Opera** (www.nationalopera.gr; 🕿), also based here.

Stavros Niarchos Park

Athens is short on green spaces, so **Stavros Niarchos Park** (Map p82; www.snfcc.org) is a true breath of fresh air.

A large central lawn hosts free dance and exercise classes, as well as midnight movie marathons in summer, while rambling paths cut through patches of lavender and rows of olive trees.

A playground, interactive sound installations and rental bikes (€1 per hour, €3 to register the first time) add to the fun.

★ Top Tips

○ Be sure you're on a Faliro-bound tram, as the line splits near the sea.

○ In addition to public transport, the Stavros Niarchos Foundation runs a shuttle bus from Syntagma, nine to 11 times daily from about 8.30am to 10pm.

○ The waterfront along the Faliro tramline is rocky, but some people do swim. Get off the tram at Mousson for the easiest water access. You can also continue along to Glyfada, Voula and Vouliagmeni.

✕ Take a Break

There are two cafes and a bistro, open till midnight, in Stavros Niarchos Park, and some restaurants and snacks in Flisvos Park. You could also continue to Piraeus for dinner at Michelin-starred **Varoulko** (www.varoulko.gr).

Survival Guide

The station at the port of Piraeus UNGVARI ATTILA/SHUTTERSTOCK ©

Before You Go

Book Your Stay

o Athens offers the full range of options.

o In the midrange shoot for one of the new breed of high-design suites in the Syntagma, Monastiraki and Psyrri areas.

o Book two months ahead for best selection; for summer, four months ahead.

o Pools are scarce, and wi-fi can be sluggish even in high-end places.

Useful Website

o **Boutique Athens** (www.boutiqueathens. com) Spacious apartments and whole houses all over town.

Best Budget

Acropolis Select (www. acropoliselect.gr) Budget travellers deserve rooftop Acropolis-view breakfasts too.

City Circus (www. citycircus.gr) Win Ins-

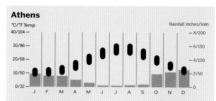

Athens

When to Go

o **Summer (Jun–Aug)** Peak heat and prices, but great outdoor festivals and street life. Athenians leave in August; some bars and shops close. (Also applies to Easter.)

o **Autumn (Sep–Oct)** Milder temps, thinner crowds. Accommodation prices usually drop by 20%.

o **Winter (Nov–Mar)** Cooler, with occasional rain or snow. Lively arts and nightlife. Cheapest lodging, but can be chilly.

o **Spring (Apr–May)** Ideal weather, few crowds. Reasonable accommodation, and, in May, outdoor cinemas and restaurants start to open.

tagram with #hostellife pics from this hip spot.

Marble House Pension (www.marblehouse.gr) Wave to the neighbours on the alley.

Phaedra (www. hotelphaedra.com) A family-run institution on a prime corner in Plaka.

Best Midrange

InnAthens (www.inn athens.com) Excellent value for such good style and location.

Pamé House (www.

pamehouse.com) Slick entry in Psyrri scene.

Lozenge (www.lozenge hotel.com) Quiet and chic, for a good price in a prime area.

Coco-Mat Hotels (www.athensbc.com) Several mod hotels, in the Acropolis area and Kolonaki.

Best Top End

Athens Was (www. athenswas.gr) No better location for visiting the Acropolis.

Accommodation by Neighbourhood

Neighbourhood	For	Against
Plaka	Atmosphere. Close to Acropolis.	Definitely tourist central.
Syntagma	Larger rooms with best amenities.	Big 1970s buildings can be characterless.
Monastiraki & Psyrri	Scenic, easiest metro access from airport.	Noise from bars, open till 4am on weekends.
Acropolis Area	Local vibe in Makrygianni and Koukaki.	Koukaki is a 15-minute walk to the Acropolis.
Kolonaki	Quiet and chic. Convenient to museums.	Long walk or short metro ride to Plaka.
Omonia	Some good new and renovated hotels.	Visible drug use and prostitution at night.
Exarhia	Vibrant nightlife and restaurants.	Few hotels. Far from central sights.
Thisio & Petralona	Pleasant, modern. Very few tourists.	Few hotels, and 10- to 15-minute walk to Acropolis.
Mets & Pangrati	Quiet, with good restaurants.	Less convenient locale. Reach Acropolis by bus or 20-minute walk.
Gazi, Keramikos & Metaxourgio	Athens' hipster fringes, with good bars.	Gazi is loud. Eastern end of Metaxourgio is seedy.

Grande Bretagne (www.grandebretagne.gr) Athens' grande dame.

Electra Palace (www.electrahotels.gr) 'Palace' is well earned.

Project 3 Urban Chic Hotel (www.project3urbanchichotel.com) Fab location near Kolonaki's main square.

Arriving in Athens

Eleftherios Venizelos International Airport

Athens' **airport** (www.aia.gr), at Spata, 27km east of Athens, is a manageable terminal with all modern amenities.

Transport Options

Metro Line 3 One-way/return within seven days €9/16, 50 minutes to Monastiraki, every 30 minutes between 6.30am and 11.30pm

Bus X95 €5.50, one hour to 1½ hours to Syntagma, every 20 to 30 minutes, 24 hours

Taxi Flat fare to centre, tolls included, day/night €40/55, 30 to 45 minutes. Night fare applies to drop-off time, not pickup.

Welcome Pickups (www.welcomepickups.com) Book ahead, at a higher price than taxis.

Port of Piraeus

o Most island ferries and all cruise ships arrive at **Piraeus** (www.olp.gr), southwest of Athens.

o Free shuttle buses run inside the huge port zone and stop across the road from the metro.

o **Greek Ferries** (www.greekferries.gr) Schedules and tickets, or check www.openseas.gr.

Transport Options

Metro Line 1 €1.20, 30 minutes to Thissio, 5.30am to midnight

Bus X80 From the cruise-ship port to major sites, €4.50, 30 minutes to the Acropolis, May to October only

Bus 040 To Syntagma, €1.20, every 30 minutes, 24 hours

Night bus 500 To Omonia, €1.20, 45 min-

utes, hourly midnight to 5am

Taxi Drivers waiting in front of the metro are notorious for overcharging. Hail from the street if possible. Expect to pay €20 to €25, on the meter, to the centre.

Getting Around

Metro

o Line 1 (green, to Piraeus), Line 2 (red), Line 3 (blue, to the airport, though some trains end a few stops earlier).

o Maps have clear icons and English labels. All stations have elevators and wheelchair access.

o Trains operate from 5.30am to midnight, every five or six minutes during peak periods and every 10 minutes off-peak. Last airport train is 11pm. On Friday and Saturday, lines 2 and 3 run till 2am.

o Information: www.stasy.gr.

Taxi

o Short trips around central Athens cost about €6.

o Normal tariff is marked '1' on the meter; after midnight and holidays, the tariff is '2', about 60% higher.

o If a taxi picks you up while already carrying passengers, each person pays the fare on the meter minus any diversions to drop others (note what it's at when you get in).

o To the airport, drivers often propose a flat fare of €45/60 during the day/night, about the same as the meter with all legitimate add-ons (tolls, airport fee, luggage fees).

o For street hailing, thrust your arm out vigorously and shout your destination.

o Taxi apps ease many difficulties: **Beat** (www.thebeat.co/gr), **Taxiplon** (www.taxiplon.gr).

o For day trips, **Athens Tour Taxi** (www.athenstourtaxi.com) is recommended.

Bus

○ Typical service is every 15 minutes, 5am to midnight.

○ For directions and routes, use Google Maps or the trip planner at the website of the bus company, **OASA** (www.oasa.gr), also at http://telematics.oasa.gr.

○ Useful lines for tourists are electric trolleybuses 2, 5, 11 and 15, from Syntagma to the National Archaeological Museum.

Tram

○ The tramline runs from Syntagma, opposite the National Gardens, to the coast, then splits: east to Voula (one hour) and west to Faliro (45 minutes) and Piraeus (one hour).

○ Service is from 5.30am to midnight Sunday to Thursday (every 10 minutes), and to 2.30am on Friday and Saturday (every 40 minutes).

○ Ticket machines are on the platforms.

○ Information: www.stasy.gr.

Bicycle

○ No cycle lanes, reckless drivers and loads

Transport Options

Walking Central Athens is compact. Likely what you'll do the most.

Metro Fast, efficient, most useful for visitors.

Taxi Affordable. Drivers speak patchy English.

Bus Go everywhere, but no printed maps.

Tram Slow but scenic way to the coast.

Car Unnecessary and stressful, due to narrow streets and congestion; avoid.

of hills. But some hardy locals do ride, and sightseeing by bike can be efficient (and breezy).

○ A bike route runs from Thisio to the coast. **Roll in Athens** (www.rollinathens.tours) leads good tours.

○ For bicycle hire, see **Funky Ride** (Map p46; www.funkyride.gr).

Essential Information

Accessible Travel

○ The 2004 Paralympic Games improved accessibility, but marble and stepped alleys are challenging for wheelchairs.

○ Visual and hearing impairments are rarely catered to, but there are tactile sidewalk strips.

○ Download Lonely Planet's free **Accessible Travel Online Resources** guide from https://shop.lonelyplanet.com/categories/accessible-travel.com.

Matt Barrett's Greece Guides (www.greece-travel.com/handicapped) Local articles, resorts and tour groups.

Sage Traveling (www.sagetraveling.com/athens-accessible-travel) A wheelchair rider's experience.

Extramilers (www.extramilers.eu) New and expanding travellers' resource for those with disabilities.

National Confederation of Persons with Disabilities (www.esamea.gr) Athens-based advocacy organisation.

Perpato (www.per pato.gr) Accessibility advocacy organisation based in northern Greece.

European Disability Forum (www.edf-feph.org) Vast clearinghouse of European-wide initiatives for people with disabilities.

Business Hours

o Some restaurants and bars scale back opening days in winter.

o Live-music bars without outdoor space usually shut for the whole summer.

o Many smaller businesses and shops close for an hour or two in the afternoon.

o As a general rule:

Banks 8.30am–2.30pm Monday to Thursday, 8am–2pm Friday

Cafes 9am–midnight

Bars 6pm–2am or 4am

Clubs 10pm–4am

Restaurants noon–10pm or later

Shops 8am–3pm Monday, Wednesday and Saturday; 8am–2.30pm and 5–8pm Tuesday, Thursday and Friday

Discount Cards

Athens Spotlighted (www.athenspotlighted.gr) From the Athens Airport Information Desk or register online. Discounts at some shops, restaurants and a few sights. Free.

European Youth Card (www.eyca.org) Ages 13 to 30. Need not be a resident of Europe. €14.

International Student Identity Card (ISIC; www.isic.org) Students over age 12. US$4-25.

Tickets & Passes

The reloadable paper **Ath.ena Ticket** works on buses, the tram and the metro. Buy from machines or offices in the metro. (A plastic Ath.ena Card is also available, only from ticket offices.) Ath.ena Tickets issued for express buses (from the airport, for example) cannot be reloaded. You need a special ticket for airport services – they are not covered by regular tickets.

Single ticket (90 minutes, unlimited transfers)	€1.20
24-hour pass	€4.10
Five-day pass	€8.20
Three-day pass with round-trip airport ticket	€20

Children under six travel free. Under 18 or over 65 are half-fare, but you must buy at a ticket office.

On the metro, tap the card at the turnstiles. On buses and trams, board at any door and tap on the validation machine.

Dos & Don'ts

Body language 'Yes' is a swing of the head and 'no' is a quick raising of the head or eyebrows, often accompanied by a 'tsk'.

Eating If invited out, do offer to pay, but don't insist (it is an honour to pay for dinner, so you should do it, too). Don't rush dinner or the waitstaff.

Photography Inside churches, don't take photos, especially of the altar or icons. At archaeological sites, using a tripod marks you as a professional and may require special permission.

Places of worship Cover shoulders and knees. Some churches will deny admission if you're showing too much skin.

Seniors Card-carrying EU pensioners.

Electricity

Type F
230V/50Hz

Type C
220V/50Hz

Emergencies & Police

Emergency	112
Police	100
Tourist Police	171

If calling from a non-Greek number, only 112 connects.

Central Police Station (210 770 5711, emergency 100; www.astynomia.gr; Leoforos Alexandras 173; M Ambelokipi)

Syntagma Police Station (210 725 7005, emergency 100; Mimnermou 6-8; M Syntagma) Most convenient for visitors.

Tourist Police Station (210 920 0724, 24hr 171; Veïkou 43-45; 8am-10pm; M Sygrou-Fix, Akropoli)

Health

Check pharmacy windows for details of the nearest duty pharmacy, or call 1434

(Greek only). There's a 24-hour pharmacy at the airport.

SOS Doctors (☎ 210 821 2222, 1016; www. sosiatroi.gr; ⊙24hr) English-speaking doctors who make house (or hotel) calls.

Internet Access

○ Most hotels have internet access and wi-fi, though it is not always very fast.

○ Free wireless hot spots are at Syntagma, Thisio, Gazi and the port of Piraeus.

○ Cosmote (Greece's main telecommunications company) maintains public data hot spots; buy prepaid cards or SIM cards (bring a passport) at Cosmote or Germanos stores.

Left Luggage

There is reasonably priced (from €6/six hours) storage at the airport (www.care-4bag.gr), and most hotels store luggage free for guests. Also:

Athens Lockers (www. athenslockers.com)

LeaveYourLuggage. gr (www.leaveyourluggage. gr; 🛜)

Or check www. thisisathens.org for others.

Money

○ Shops and restaurants are required to have card payment systems, but cash is still far more commonly used.

○ Major banks have branches around Syntagma. ATMs are plentiful enough in commercial districts, but harder to find in more residential areas.

National Bank of Greece Has a 24-hour automated exchange machine.

Onexchange Currency and money transfers. Branches include **Syntagma** (www.onexchange. gr) and **Monastiraki** (www.onexchange.gr).

Tipping

Hotels and Ferries Bellhops and stewards expect a small gratuity of €1 to €3.

Restaurants If a service charge is included, just round up the bill. If no service charge, leave 10% to 20%.

Taxis Round up the fare by a euro or two. There's a small fee for

handling bags; this is an official charge, not a tip.

Post

The Greek postal system is slow. Larger post offices sell boxes for shipping.

Athens Central Post Office (www.elta.gr)

Public Holidays

All banks and shops, most museums and ancient sites close on these holidays, as well as Orthodox holidays (like Greek Easter), with movable dates.

New Year's Day 1 January

Epiphany 6 January

Greek Independence Day 25 March

Labour Day (Protomagia) 1 May

Feast of the Assumption 15 August

Ohi Day 28 October

Christmas Day 25 December

St Stephen's Day 26 December

Safe Travel

○ Since the financial crisis, crime has risen. But

Greek Orthodox Holidays

These are all official holidays, and many people take the full week preceding Easter as a vacation. Book hotels and travel well in advance.

Year	First Monday in Lent	Good Friday to Easter Monday	Pentecost Monday
2023	27 February	14–17 April	5 June
2024	18 March	3–6 May	24 June
2025	3 March	18–21 April	9 June
2026	23 February	10–13 April	1 June

this is a rise from almost zero, and violent street crime remains rare.

o Be aware of surroundings at night, especially southwest of Omonia, where prostitutes and drug users gather.

o Phone snatching is on the rise. Don't stand on the street absorbed in your phone or leave it on restaurant tables.

o Pickpockets operate especially on the metro green line (Piraeus–Kifisia), around Omonia and Athinas and at the Monastiraki Flea Market.

o Scammers target solo male travellers. Be wary of invitations to bars, which can end in exorbitant bills and/or adulterated drinks.

Strikes

o Strikes and demonstrations can disrupt public transport and close sights and shops, but they are almost always announced in advance.

o Given the frequency of strikes, travel insurance is recommended.

o Check for strikes at www.apergia.gr or the US Embassy (https://gr.usembassy.gov).

Smoking

An estimated 24% of Greek adults smoke. Smoking in enclosed public places is banned, but this is often unheeded in bars. Outdoor seating is well used by smokers. Vaping is not very common.

Telephone

o Country code: 30.

o Athens landline numbers begin with 21; mobile numbers with 6.

o Public phones allow international calls. Buy cards at kiosks (periptera).

o SIM cards are reasonably priced. Buy at major phone shops. You must show your passport.

o US/Canadian phones must have a dual- or tri-band system; make sure phones are carrier unlocked before leaving.

Toilets

o Public toilets are rare. If you use a cafe, it's polite to buy something.

o Greek plumbing is fragile and does not accommodate toilet paper. It should be placed in the bin next to the toilet.

Best Insights

Understand contemporary Athens with these books, films and songs.

Walking in Athens with Constantine Cavafy Explore the Athens of today by comparing it to the Athens of the turn of the 20th century.

Never on Sunday (1960) Piraeus prostitute with a heart of gold (Melina Mercouri) meets fussy American classicist (Jules Dassin).

Uncle Petros and Goldbach's Conjecture (Apostolos Doxiadis; 1992) Tale of love, mathematics and Athens.

Attenberg (2010) Athina Rachel Tsangari's ode to disaffected youth.

Rembetika: Songs of the Greek Underground 1925–1947 Many of the classic songs you're likely to hear played in bars these days.

Tora Tora (Boro Boro) (Giorgos Mazonakis and Arash; 2022) Summer anthem of the lovelorn by veteran Piraeus-area singer and Iranian-Swedish singer.

Tourist Information

● Check the City of Athens culture website (https://cultureisathens.gr) for what's on in town.

Athens City Information Airport (www.thisisathens.org)

Athens City Informa-tion Syntagma (www.thisisathens.org)

EOT (Greek National Tourism Organisation; www.visitgreece.gr)

Visas

Australia, Canada, Israel, Japan, New Zealand and USA No visa required for tourist visits of up to 90 days.

EU No visa required.

Other countries Check with a Greek embassy or consulate.

Water

Tap water is safe to drink.

Language

Greek is believed to be one of the oldest European languages, with an oral tradition of 4000 years and a written tradition of approximately 3000 years.

The Greek alphabet can look a bit intimidating if you're used to the Roman alphabet, but with a bit of practice you'll start recognising the characters quickly. If you read our pronunciation guides as if they were English, you'll be understood.

To enhance your trip with a phrasebook, visit lonelyplanet.com.

Basics

Hello

Γειά σας   *ya·sas* (polite)
Γειά σου   *ya·su* (informal)

Good morning/evening.

Καλή μέρα/   *ka·li me·ra/*
σπέρα   *spe·ra*

Goodbye

Αντίο   *an·di·o*

Yes./No

Ναι./Οχι.   *ne/o·hi*

Please

Παρακαλώ   *pa·ra·ka·lo*

Thank you

Ευχαριστώ   *ef·ha·ri·sto*

Sorry

Συγγνώμη   *sigh·no·mi*

What's your name?

Πώς σας λένε;   *pos sas le·ne*

My name is ...

Με λένε …   *me le·ne ...*

Do you speak English?

Μιλάτε αγγλικά; *mi·la·te an·gli·ka*

I (don't) understand

(Δεν)   *(dhen)*
καταλαβαίνω   *ka·ta·la·ve·no*

Eating & Drinking

I'd like ...	Θα ήθελα …	*tha i·the·la...*
a cup of coffee	ένα φλυτζάνι καφέ	*e·na fli·dza·ni ka·fe*
a table	ένα τραπέζι	*e·na tra·pe·zi*
for two	για δύο α άτομα	*ya dhi·o a·to·ma*
one beer	μία μπύρα	*mi·a bi·ra*

I'm a vegetarian

Είμαι χορτοφάγος
i·me hor·to·fa·ghos

What would you recommend?

Τι θα συνιστούσες;
ti tha si·ni·stu·ses

Cheers!

Εις υγείαν!
is i·yi·an

That was delicious.

Ήταν νοστιμότατο
i·tan no·sti·mo·ta·to

Please bring the bill

Το λογαριασμό, παρακαλώ
to lo·ghar·ya·zmo pa·ra·ka·lo

Shopping

I'd like to buy ...
Θέλω ν' αγοράσω ...
the·lo na·gho·ra·so ...

I'm just looking
Απλώς κοιτάζ.
ap·los ki·ta·zo

How much is it?
Πόσο κάνει;
po·so ka·ni

It's too expensive
Είναι πολύ ακριβ.
i·ne po·li a·kri·vo

Can you lower the price?

Μπορείς να	*bo·ris na*
κατεβάσεις	*ka·te·va·sis*
την τιμή;	*tin ti·mi*

Emergencies

Help!
Βοήθεια!
vo·i·thya

Call a doctor!
Φωνάξτε ένα γιατρό!
fo·nak·ste e·na yi·a·tro

Call the police!
Φωνάξτε την αστυνομία!
fo·nak·ste tin a·sti·no·mi·a

There's been an accident
Εγινε ατύχημα
ey·i·ne a·ti·hi·ma

I'm ill   Είμαι άρρωστος
i·me a·ro·stos

It hurts here. Πονάει εδώ
po·na·i·e·dho

I'm lost   Έχω χαθεί
e·kho kha·thi

Time & Numbers

What time is it?
Τι ώρα είναι*ti o·ra i·ne*

It's (two o'clock)
Είναι (δύο η ώρα)
i·ne (dhi·o i o·ra)

yesterday χθες   *hthes*

today σήμερα   *si·me·ra*

tomorrow αύριο   *av·ri·o*

morning πρωί   *pro·i*

afternoon απόγευμα
a·po·yev·ma

evening βράδυ   *vra·dhi*

1	ένας/μία	
	e·nas/mi·a (m/f)	
	ένα	*e·na* (n)
2	δύο	*dhi·o*
3	τρεις	*tris* (m&f)
	τρία	*tri·a* (n)
4		τέσσερεις
	te·se·ris (m&f)	
		τέσσερα
	te·se·ra (n)	
5	πέντε	*pen·de*
6	έξη	*e·xi*
7	επτά	*ep·ta*
8	οχτώ	*och·to*
9	εννέα	*e·ne·a*
10	δέκα	*dhe·ka*

Transport & Directions

Where is ...?
Πού είναι ...;
pu i·ne ...

What's the address?
Ποια είναι η
διεύθυνση;
dhi·ef·thin·si

Can you show me (on the map)?
Μπορείς να μου
bo·ris na mu
δείξεις (στο χάρτη);
dhik·sis (sto khar·ti)

I want to go to ...
Θέλω να πάω στο/στη ...
the·lo na pao sto/sti ...

Where do I buy a ticket?
Πού αγοράζω εισιτήριο;
pu a·gho·ra·zo i·si·ti·ri·o

What time does it leave?
Τι ώρα φεύγει;
ti o·ra fev·yi

Does it stop at ...?
Σταματάει στο ...;
sta·ma·ta·i sto ...

I'd like to get off at ...
Θα ήθελα να κατεβώ ...
tha i·the·la na ka·te·vo ...

Behind the Scenes

Send Us Your Feedback

We love to hear from travellers – your comments help make our books better. We read every word, and we guarantee that your feedback goes straight to the authors. Visit **lonelyplanet.com/contact** to submit your updates and suggestions.

Note: We may edit, reproduce and incorporate your comments in Lonely Planet products such as guidebooks, websites and digital products, so let us know if you don't want your comments reproduced or your name acknowledged. For a copy of our privacy policy visit lonelyplanet.com/privacy.

Acknowledgements

Front cover photograph: Statues of the Acropolis, Stefan Brueckner/EyeEm/Getty ©
Back cover photograph: Koulouri, Athens, Adél Békefi/Getty ©

Alexis' Thanks

Boundless appreciation of the people of Athens for their help in researching and learning about their wonderful city, which I have continued to do for decades, with no end in sight. Ryan is a peachy companion, on the road and off. Anthy, Costas and Matthew first introduced me to Greece and help make it my home, for which I am forever grateful. Great thanks, too, to Zora O'Neill and Simon Richmond for previous iterations of this book.

This Book

This 6th edition of Lonely Planet's *Pocket Athens* guidebook was researched and written by Alexis Averbuck. The previous edition was written by Zora O'Neill. This guidebook was produced by the following:

Commissioning Editor
Kate Chapman

Production Editor
Graham O'Neill

Cartographer
Julie Dodkins

Book Designer
Nicolas D'Hoedt

Assisting Editors
Bridget Blair,
Anne Mulvaney

Cover Researcher
Hannah Blackie

Thanks to
Ronan Abayawickrema,
Alex Conroy, Charlotte Orr

Index

See also separate subindexes for:

Eating p188
Drinking p189
Entertainment p190
Shopping p190

Sights 000
Map Pages **000**